GUIDE TO

MARYLAND TROUT FISHING

The Catch-and-Release Streams

by Charlie Gelso & Larry Coburn

Published by K&D Limited, Inc.
14834 Old Frederick Road
Woodbine, MD 21797
410-489-4967 • Email rivrmyst@bellatlantic.net

Printed in the United States of America

Painting on front cover is an original by Mark Susinno

ISBN 1-893342-02-6

Library of Congress Cataloging-in-Publication Data

Gelso, Charles J., 1941-
    Guide to Maryland trout fishing: the catch and release streams / by Charlie Gelso & Larry Coburn.
        p. cm.
    Includes bibliographical references.
    ISBN 1-893342-02-6
    1. Trout fishing--Maryland--Guidebooks. 1. Maryland--Guidebooks. I. Title: Maryland trout fishing. II. Coburn, Larry, 1957-III. Title

Cover and text design/typesetting by
Donna J. Dove, K&D Limited, Inc.

Preface

This book is about the streams and rivers in Maryland that have catch-and-release regulations on them. Several of these streams have strict catch-and-release policies, whereas others have delayed harvest regulations (which are being used more and more in recent years). The streams that we write about have one or more sections that are under such special regulations (rather than the entire stream), and our focus is on those sections. Not surprisingly, the streams with special regulations are the premiere trout waters in the state. These are the waters with the best habitat, and they support substantial trout populations. Most also contain wild (streambred) trout, or at least trout that will "hold over," surviving the warm Maryland summers.

Just a few short years ago, this book could not have been written. There were not enough streams with special regulation sections to allow for more than a small pamphlet. In recent years, however, Maryland trout fishing has come into its own. New catch-and-release sections have been created on several streams and rivers, including delayed harvest regulations on some, and even reverse delayed harvest on one stream (Owens Creek). Many of the streams with special regulation sections are tailwaters. Although we recognize that there is some controversy surrounding the value of tailwaters, it is clear that some rivers have been brought to life because of wise water release policies from dams and reservoirs. To those who complain that tailwaters are not truly wild, we simply point to rivers like the Savage, the Gunpowder, and the North Branch of the Potomac as examples of blue ribbon rivers that have been wonderfully affected by such water release policies and have all the feel of a wild river.

Our aim in this book is to provide a clear picture of each stream and to aid the angler in his or her fishing efforts on that water. For each stream, we offer a description; discuss the characteristics of the trout that inhabit it and how to fish for those trout; note the tackle and equipment that are appropriate; describe hatches, other stream life, and effective fly patterns; point to some of the key problems; and tell you how to get there. A big part of getting you there is a good, clear map, and we have sought to create the very best maps possible. In presenting this information, a main goal has been to offer useful and interesting information, without getting the reader lost in details. You, the reader, will of course be the ultimate judge of the extent to which we have succeeded.

Although this book is clearly oriented toward fly fishing, we believe it will be useful to spin fishers also. Only two stream sections in the book (Big Hunting Creek and one section of the Savage River) prohibit spin fishing. Stream descriptions, discussions of stocking policies and the trout in each river, as well as the maps and directions should be every bit as pertinent to spin fishers as fly anglers.

You will note that we divide the book into the central Maryland streams and the rivers of western Maryland. The novice angler or the fisherman from out of state may wonder what happened to the eastern region. Stated simply, there are no catch-and-release streams in eastern Maryland, as the prime trout waters are from the central region westward.

A thread running through this guide pertains to the many improvements that have taken place in recent times in Maryland trout fishing. This theme is seen most sharply in the beginning chapter on the Gunpowder and final chapter on the North Branch of the Potomac. It also appears in many of the chapters in between. These positive developments have been due to the wise and tireless efforts of many people — members of conservation and fishing organizations such as Trout Unlimited, Maryland Fly Anglers, and others. We also believe Maryland has one of the most enlightened Departments of Natural Resources anywhere, and in many ways this book is a tribute to their exemplary work. As we have observed the scene, Bob Bachman has been a major force in coldwater management in the state. He provided wise and creative leadership to coldwater fisheries development during his years with the DNR, and now Bob Lunsford has continued ably in Bachman's tradition, adding his own creative energy to development of trout fisheries. Central and Western Regional Managers, Charlie Gougeon and Ken Pavol and their staffs, have made huge contributions, in our estimation, over many years. So, too, has trout specialist and biologist, Howard Stinefelt. We don't think the state could have a better group of folks at DNR.

There are many people to whom we owe a debt of gratitude in our work on this book. Jay Sheppard has been our fly fishing mentor over many years, and his influence appears throughout these pages. Jay, a biologist by training, is the most knowledgeable fly angler we know; and he has been more than willing to respond to our many questions over a lot of years. Most recently, he helped a great deal in our study of the western Maryland rivers. Charlie Gougeon and Ken Pavol, noted above, have made significant input into our work on the central and western region streams, respectively. Some great insights were offered by Frank Ryan on Morgan Run, Rob Gilford on Big Hunting Creek, John Mullican on Owens Creek, Don Hershfeld on the Youghioghenny River, and Dick Sluss on Town Creek. And Susan Rivers, DNR specialist in entomology, offered enlightening insect information on several rivers. All of these individuals provided time and great information, and thankfully, if they felt imposed upon, they surely never showed it!

Our publisher, Donna Dove, who operates K & D Limited, has been incredibly helpful in editing our work and offering advice about presentation and other aspects of publication, and in promoting our work. It mattered much to us that our work mattered to Donna.

Finally, we want to acknowledge our wives, Jean and Donna, and our kids (some of them grown), Phil, Chuck, Brett, Catherine, Marie, Ryan, and Heather. We could not have written this book without their support. (At times each of them has gone fishing with us, too.) Nor could we have done all the necessary "background research" that naturally had to be done over many years without their understanding and encouragement.

— C.G & L.C. October 1999

TABLE OF CONTENTS

PART I

THE RIVERS AND STREAMS OF CENTRAL MARYLAND

CHAPTER 1
GUNPOWDER FALLS
From Rags to Riches

I n the not-too-distant past, Gunpowder Falls might have been rightfully considered a biological wasteland. It was a tailwater, and the water release policy from the dam at Prettyboy Reservoir seemed to be dictated by just about everything but fisheries enhancement. At times the water was essentially turned off at the dam. The flows got so low, and the temperatures so warm, that trout had little or no chance of survival. The river was managed as a put-and-take fishery, with spring stocking followed by intense fishing pressure, and few trout surviving after the spring. Those that avoided the frying pan were then done in by the low flows and high temperatures of Maryland summers.

All of that was before 1986. At that time, after several years of work by the Maryland Chapter of Trout Unlimited, a water release agreement was negotiated with the City of Baltimore. The agreement, which must be periodically renewed, called for a minimum flow of water and a coldwater release policy. The result was a flow that is never too low for fish survival (a minimum of 11.5 cubic feet per second), and water temperatures that range from about the mid-40s to the lower 60s. In fact, the water can be so chilly during hot summer days that we have playfully suggested that the Gunpowder is the only river around in which an angler can get hypothermia and sunstroke at the same time! The long and short of this is that the wise water release policy, along with good fisheries management, has turned a biological wasteland into a blue ribbon trout fishery.

This tailwater, located in Baltimore County, contains many miles of fishable water. The catch-and-release section begins at Prettyboy Dam, and proceeds for 7.2 miles before it passes Blue Mount Road. Only flies and artificial lures are permitted. Below Blue Mount Road, the regulation changes to two fish per day (bait fishing permitted) for the next 4.2 miles to Corbett Road. Finally, from Corbett Road to the Loch Raven Reservoir, the river is managed as a put-and-take fishery, with a limit of 5 fish per day and no bait restrictions. Our focus in this chapter will be on the catch-and-release section, but much of what we have to say also applies to the waters downstream of Blue Mount Road.

The Gunpowder is one of the bigger rivers in Maryland. Its width varies from about 30' to more than 70', with an average of about 45-50'. There are many holes that are 4-6' deep. Diversity characterizes this river and its many faces. The stream is nestled in a valley, which at points is steep enough to be considered a miniature canyon. There is just about every kind of water anyone could think of:

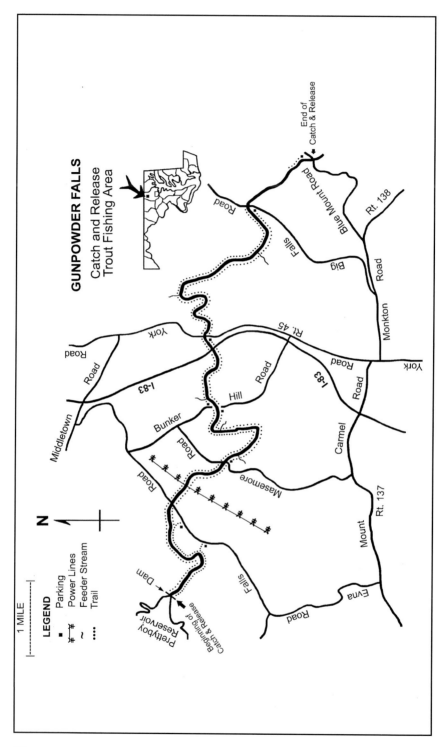

GUNPOWDER FALLS

Catch and Release
Trout Fishing Area

LEGEND

■ Parking
✠ Power Lines
~ Feeder Stream
⋯ Trail

1 MILE

N

riffles, runs, pools, flats, undercut banks, fast and slow water, high and low gradient, and more.

As you can see from our map, the catch-and-release section contains six access points, but the character of river really can be divided into two dramatically different types. The upper section, from Prettyboy down to Falls Road is high gradient, with many fast chutes and riffles, and occasional log jams. The bottom is very rocky, and the wading can be treacherous. In fact, we fish portions of this section from the bank and from large rocks along the bank. When we wade, we do so very carefully. The rocks so often seem hard to negotiate, and their contours unpredictable. This is classic rainbow trout water, although rainbows have all but disappeared from it (see *The Fish and The Fishing*).

The lower section, on the other hand, is slower moving, with more pools, undercut banks, root systems, along with some great flats. The bottom is largely gravel. This section looks more like a Piedmont region stream than does the upper section. Although the flow can be heavy (and always feels heavier than it looks), the gravel bottom usually makes for very comfortable wading. This gravel also provides great spawning habitat for the brown trout that are thriving in the lower section.

Traversing almost 20,000 acres of largely public land, the Gunpowder is one of the most scenic rivers in Maryland. Clients we guide on this river always seem to be taken by the river's beauty and the sense of wilderness created by its surroundings. The upper section stirs the image of a rugged, brawling western river; the beauty of the lower section, on the other hand, is more tranquil and mellow. Common to both, though, is the sense of being away from it all. You will run into no houses on this stream, but you will encounter a range of wildlife and forestation. At the same time, most of the river is accompanied by good paths. All things considered, it is probably most accurate to describe the Gunpowder and its surroundings as a "civilized wilderness."

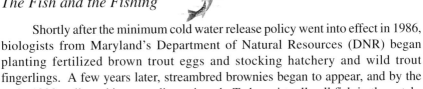

The Fish and the Fishing

Shortly after the minimum cold water release policy went into effect in 1986, biologists from Maryland's Department of Natural Resources (DNR) began planting fertilized brown trout eggs and stocking hatchery and wild trout fingerlings. A few years later, streambred brownies began to appear, and by the early 1990s, all stocking was discontinued. Today, virtually all fish in the catch-and-release section are wild fish, except for the few who migrate several miles upriver from the stocked sections below Corbett Road.

The Gunpowder contains browns, rainbows, and native brookies. Over the years, the brown trout population has grown tremendously, and estimates based on electroshocking suggest that over 95% of all trout are now browns. There is some limited reproduction of rainbows, mostly in the section above Falls Road. As we have said, that section is classic rainbow water, so one might expect more reproduction of rainbows there. The problem, though, according to DNR biologist, Charlie Gougeon, is that there is limited spawning habitat in this section, so the rainbows cannot reproduce much. Brookies, on the other hand, typically spawn in small feeder streams to the Gunpowder, and then some will migrate into the river.

There is a high density of trout in the Gunpowder. For example, Charlie Gougeon has reported brown trout densities as high as 1500-1600 adult trout per mile in the upper part of the River, along with rainbow densities of over 200 per mile in this same general area. The densities are less as one moves downstream, and are lowest in the Blue Mount Road area. But don't be fooled by this statement. There are plenty of trout throughout the catch-and-release stretch (as well as the two per day stretch from Blue Mount Road to Corbett Road), and as you move into pieces of water where there are *relatively* fewer fish, you also find many less anglers.

Trout in the Gunpowder range in size from about 8-14". Occasionally, you find some real submarines. Wally Vait, who owns a quality fly shop (called "On the Fly") near the River, probably knows more about the Gunpowder's subtleties than anyone around. In slide presentations that he makes, Wally shows some pictures of large spawning brown trout. These 18" fish in one of his slides are dwarfed by a much larger trout, one that Wally estimates to be in the mid-twenties range!

One distinctive feature of the Gunpowder trout is that they are fighters. Ten-inch trout fight like much bigger fish. Charlie (Gelso) was struck by this in the summer of 1998, when he fished the Clark's Fork of the Yellowstone River in Montana. The Clark's Fork is inhabited by fish about the same size as those in the Gunpowder, and they are all streambred (rainbows, cutthroats, and brookies). But there was no comparison between the fight they put up compared to Gunpowder trout. Surprisingly, the Gunpowder browns can be acrobatic leapers. We say "surprisingly" because brown trout are not known to be leapers, as are rainbows.

Another distinctive feature of Gunpowder trout is how they take surface flies. The trout seem to sit on or near the bottom. They then dart to the surface and whack the fly — and spit it out almost instantly, if you give them the split second to discover that they've just eaten a fake. Thus, to catch these critters, the angler must be always alert, and time the strike just right. Surface "sippers" (trout that sit near the top and just tilt their heads up to sip surface flies) do appear in a few slow pools and eddies, but they are much less common than one might expect on this river.

The wild trout on the Gunpowder are challenging. Because of the quality of the fishing and the hatches (see *Hatches*), the River now gets fairly heavy fishing pressure. The fish are pretty educated, so you have to fish them wisely and effec-tively to have success. Do not go to the Gunpowder expecting 20 fish days. This is a river where you earn the fish you catch, and should view every one of these gamers as a prize. Don't get us wrong. We have had some great days on this river, as have our clients. But the norm is to catch a few fish, *and* for the fishing to be extremely interesting and enjoyable when all things are considered.

One of the many characters of the Gunpowder River.

Fishing on the surface and underneath can be equally good. In the section above Falls Road, the habitat is uniformly good, and trout seem to be everywhere. As you move downstream, you learn to pick your spots. What you typically encounter are stretches of shallow, flat water with few fish interspersed with very fishy looking holes and glides. Search for these holes and glides, and unless you see rising fish in the flat, shallow water, avoid those spots. There are some fish there, especially against the banks, but the greater densities will be found in the fishiest looking holes.

Regarding tackle, we tend to prefer longer rods on the Gunpowder. They allow for longer casts and, even more important, give you an advantage when nymphing and streamer fishing. Eight- to nine-foot rods, with line weights from 2-6 are our preference. Chest waders are recommended, although one can get by in most areas with hip boots. Given the very cold water, three millimeter neoprenes work just fine except in the dead of summer. If you use ultralights, you will usually need some insulation underneath.

One aspect of fishing the Gunpowder that should be underscored is leader and tippet sizes. Generally, when fishing the surface, longer leaders and finer tippets are preferable. Twelve foot leaders (including the tippet) and longer are best, and we rarely fish on top with tippets that are larger than 6X. Of course, this depends on water conditions. During the Hendrickson hatch in the spring, when the flows are pretty high and the flies big, we often go to 5X. When fishing underneath, we usually use 5 and 6X, depending on fly size.

The long leaders and fine tippets are important on this river for three reasons. First, the currents are very complex (much more so than at first glance), so shorter leaders will result in drag. Often this drag is barely perceptible (you can call it "microdrag"), but when it occurs, the fish rarely get fooled. The second and third reasons why light tippets are important is that the water is usually so clear, and the fish so educated. Gunpowder trout see everything that floats by, and they have doctorates in the art of detecting artificials!

As noted, there are six access points to the River. Apart from the distinctions we have made between the upper and lower sections, it is hard to differentiate these sections. Generally, the best dry fly fishing is from about a mile downstream of the York Road crossing upstream, all the way to the dam. But then again, we have had banner days on the surface below that point and have had the river to ourselves.

Speaking of having the river to yourself, as in most blue ribbon fisheries, if you want privacy, it is best to fish during the week and in the "off season." Weekends get crowded. Early winter fishing, on the other hand, can be a joy. Be careful, however, as the heart of winter begins to appear. The best fishing is upstream, closer to the dam. That is because the tailwater release produces slightly warmer water temps there in winter. The problem in winter, though, is that the rocky paths can get dangerously icy. A wading staff is a good idea. We tend to avoid the upper stretch when there is snow and ice on the paths.

Hatches, Other Stream Life, and Effective Patterns

The Gunpowder is one of the best rivers in Maryland to fish during hatch situations. There are a few especially good hatches here, although because of the cold water, hatches tend to be a little later on the Gunpowder than most freestoners.

The year begins with excellent hatches of tiny black winter stoneflies (#16-20), and this continues into early spring. (Actually, this hatch emerges around Thanksgiving, so it also "ends" the year.) A somewhat larger (#14-16) brown stonefly emerges in late winter, and overlaps with the smaller black stone. These hatches make for excellent surface fishing, and when the trout are not rising, nymphal imitations can be dynamite. Charlie's Nymph is extremely effective in this situation (see Chapter 13 for recipe).

The "April grays" represent very good hatches here. Quill Gordons (#14), little blue quills (#16-18), and Hendricksons (#10) often produce fishable hatches. The red quill (the male Henderickson) also hatches (#12-14). Note that the Hendrickson hatching on the Gunpowder is a dark Hendrickson, with slate gray wings, not the mottled wings that usually appear in fly pattern books. Dry fly patterns of the same name are the ticket when the April grays are on. You can also use an Adams of the appropriate size to imitate most of these patterns. Emerger patterns are especially effective during the Hendrickson hatch.

A range of nymphs, including the popular bead heads, can be effective at this time. We lean toward Gold-Ribbed Hare's Ears and Pheasant Tails, with the size to match just what is hatching.

A more subdued side, this long glide gives the Gunpowder River a serene look. When hatches occur, trout rise rings will pop everywhere.

The next big hatch is the sulphur hatch. Whereas the Hendricksons are on for about 2-3 weeks, the sulphurs start in about mid-May and continue into July. We think this is usually the best hatch on the Gunpowder. It is common to see sulphurs pouring off the water from early afternoon into the evening, and then for a thick spinner fall to occur at dusk. All three species of sulphurs hatch on this river. Without getting technical, we can say that the bigger versions (#14-16) hatch early in the day, and the smaller pale evening dun (#18-20) comes off in the evening. The larger sulphur tends to have a deep yellow body, sometimes with a trace of orange in it. The wings are a very light gray. The smaller sulphur has a paler body. A particularly effective sulphur pattern, Coburn's Sub Surface Sulphur (created by Larry) imitates a drowned dun (see Chapter 13).

Try staying until dark during sulphur season (you can put a note on your car that you are fishing, so the park police won't ticket you). The spinner fall, which occurs at dusk, can be spectacular! Clouds of spinners can be seen above riffles, and when they fall, the pools below those riffles will have rising fish everywhere. Beware, though, that the fishing can be maddening during this spinner fall. There are so many naturals on the water, that your imitation does not stand a great chance. Work particular fish, rather than casting to all the rises you see. After you catch or give up on that fish, move to another.

Any of a range of sulphur imitations work well. Generally, as the hatch proceeds, the fish get fussier by the day, and we move to more and more realistic (and sparser) imitations. But that, too, is not written in stone. Larry recalls one evening in mid-June when the fish seemed to take his imitations with shocking eagerness. The fly was a simple #16 sulphur imitation with no wings — just a tail, yellow body, and cream hackle wound with about six turns. During one period of several weeks when the water was unusually high, fish took only our #14 spinners during the spinner fall. The smaller flies were regularly ignored.

Regarding nymphs, hare's ears and pheasant tails are extremely effective, especially when fish are not rising. We also have had many days saved by a sulphur wet fly called the Little Marryat (#16, see Chapter 13) that we first learned about some years ago from noted Pennsylvania angler, Ed Shenck.

Summer is terrestrial time on the Gunpowder and other streams. Ants, flying ants, and beetles are effective (#16-22). Try sinking your ants if the fish will not rise to the surface. A little split shot a foot or so above the fly usually does the trick.

Midges work well, especially in pools and flats. The famous Griffith's gnat (#20-24) is our favorite, although a range of midges work. In recent years, we have seen great trico hatches (#22-24), beginning in August and continuing into the fall. The spinner fall is what you look for during this "hatch." Find clouds of tiny flies doing their mating dance above the water in mid morning, and the chances are that they are trico spinners.

Caddisflies are a main source of food, and they hatch from about April through the fall and even in early winter. In fact, they will hatch during mayfly emergences. For example, we often see an olive bodied caddis (#16) fluttering about during the sulphur hatch. And trout often prefer this caddis. There is usually a good caddis hatch in the fall, with two flies predominating: a dark olive with gray wings (#18) and a cinnamon bodied caddis with mottled wings (#16).

A caddis pattern that works well is an olive or cinnamon bodied elk wing caddis, sparsely tied. We like to hackle the fly only in the thorax, rather than throughout the body. Also, realistic caddis patterns, tied with mallard quill wings, are dynamite for the fussier fish. The Henryville Special (#14-20) is a great pattern.

The blue-winged olive (#16-20) hatches on cloudy days throughout much of the year. This "olive", though, is really not olive colored. The body is a dark gray. An #18 Adams works fine for this hatch, especially if it is sparsely tied.

The Gunpowder does not support a good minnow population. Nor does it contain great numbers of crayfish, sculpins, daces, etc. Yet patterns such as Woolly Buggers, Sculpins, Muddler Minnows, and Patuxent Specials (see Chapter 13) all work well. Classic streamers such as a Black-Nosed Dace, Mickey Finns, and Hornbergs also take fish. We tend to use these big flies (#6-12) in the colder seasons. The trick is to fish them right on the bottom. You need to feel the fly ticking the bottom, and you should expect to lose a few flies. But you will catch more fish on the bottom when, for example, woolly buggering than you will at other depths.

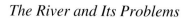

The River and Its Problems

As you can see, the Big Gunpowder has an awful lot to recommend it: A high density of fish, wild fish, fine hatches, diverse structure, and at times breathtaking scenery. While there is plenty of cover, the river is open and relatively large, so you can do some easy and long casting if you like. Because of the water release policy at the Prettyboy dam, fishing is possible year 'round. The water is never too cold or too warm for the fish and for fishing.

Although we do not see major problems with this river, there are some limitations to note. We have mentioned that the river can get crowded. Part of this crowding is what we call the "float tube hatch" and the "canoe hatch" in summer. Naturally, many tubers and canoers love this river. Although tubes and canoes only will put the fish down for a few seconds, during afternoons on the warmest days, there are at times so many tubers and canoers that the fishing stops being fun. Our recommendation: Take a break during these times.

For many of us, the virtual disappearance of rainbow trout is a limitation. After the water release policy went into effect in 1986, the DNR, along with TU support, stocked many fingerling rainbows. These fish thrived, especially in the upper section above Falls Road. Some fingerlings grew to impressive sizes. But it is clear that the river cannot sustain a sizeable wild rainbow population. Some believe, as we do, that supplemental stocking of fingerling rainbows in the upper section would greatly enhance the fishery, and result in more large fish (that seem lacking in recent years). Others argue, though, that supplemental stocking should not be done over a wild trout population. So far, the latter group has prevailed.

Sometimes it is impossible to predict how much water will be released from the Prettyboy Reservoir. During the lowest flows of Maryland summers, the water release is at times the greatest, so that the supply of drinking water is at an acceptable level in the lower Loch Raven Reservoir. The water is almost never too high to fish, but high water in fall, for example, is sometimes responsible for greatly diminished caddis hatches. It is best to check on the water level by calling *On the Fly* (410-329-6821), or checking the river report on their web site (www.onthefly.com).

Location and Access Points: How to Get There

As we have mentioned, Gunpowder Falls flows through 20,000 acres of mostly public land in Baltimore county. To get to the river, take Interstate 83 north off the Baltimore Beltway (I-695). At Exit 27, take the Hereford/Mt. Carmel Road exit. Take a left onto Mt. Carmel Road in order to go to the two upper access points (see map for specifics). To get to the four lower access points, take a right onto Mt. Carmel Road and go to York Road. A left on York Road will take you to the Bunker Hill Road area or, if you continue a mile or so, the York Road crossing. On the other hand, if you take a right on York Road, you then hang left within a few yards onto Monkton Road. This will get you to the Big Falls and Blue Mount Road sections.

As we have said, there are excellent supplies of fish in each of these sections. At the same time, each section has its own character, and each fishes a little differently. Dry fly activity tends to be best in the Masemore Road and Bunker Hill Road areas. There is great midge fishing as one gets close to the dam, as well as in certain sections sprinkled throughout the river. Note, though, that there are big exceptions to any statements that we can make about what to fish in which section. Our recommendation is that you take the time to learn this complex and fascinating river, her many twists and turns. This is truly a piece of water that becomes more endearing, even lovable, as she becomes more known and understood.

Bibliography

Gougeon, C. & Markham, J. (1998). Gunpowder Falls: The evolution of a trout fishery. htpp:/www.dnr.state.md.us/fisheries/featurestory.html.

CHAPTER 2
MORGAN RUN
A Pretty Stream With a Lot of Fish

T he Morgan Run Special Area is a three to four mile stretch of water that is within a 45 minute drive of Baltimore and a little over an hour from Washington, D. C. Although less known than the nearby Patuxent and Big Gunpowder Rivers, it contains a dense supply of trout and some of the best fishing in the state. Morgan Run is a pleasing stream for anglers at all levels of expertise. It is an especially good stream, however, for those in the early stages of their fly fishing journey.

Located in Carroll County, the catch-and-release stretch begins where Route 97 crosses the stream, and winds through wooded hills and plains until it reaches London Bridges Road. Shortly after that point, it empties into Liberty Reservoir. The stream alternates at several points throughout its life between two personalities. One is a meandering, low gradient stream, with many log jams, long pools, undercut banks and gravel bottom; the other is a faster moving, rocky bottom, and at points, boulder strewn stream, with riffles and chutes. In certain places, you could jump across the stream, and at other points it is more than 60 feet wide. Typically it is about 30 feet across. There are a good number of deep holes, as deep as 5-6'. Generally, the upper section is narrow and on the tight side for fly anglers, and the stream tends to widen as you move downstream.

Like most fly anglers, we enjoy observing nature and the beauty of trout rivers. Morgan Run does not disappoint aesthetically. This is a pretty stream. As you fish it, you will encounter a mixture of flat land and steep hills, all lined with a variety of trees, e.g., ash, maple, oak. In the spring, blooming laurel and dog-wood provide extra pleasure. There is a sense of openness, despite the small size, since Morgan Run is not canopied by trees as is, for example, the Patuxent Special Area. This openness is both a benefit and a drawback for Morgan Run. Although Morgan at times gets heavy pressure, move away from the main access points and you will have a sense of being in the woods, partaking of nature's gifts.

The Fish and the Fishing

Morgan Run is stocked each spring with both brown trout and rainbows, most in the 10-12" range, but a few much larger ones. One nice feature of the stocking practices on this stream is that local fishing groups usually float stock the fish throughout the catch-and-release stretch. This means that there are fish in just

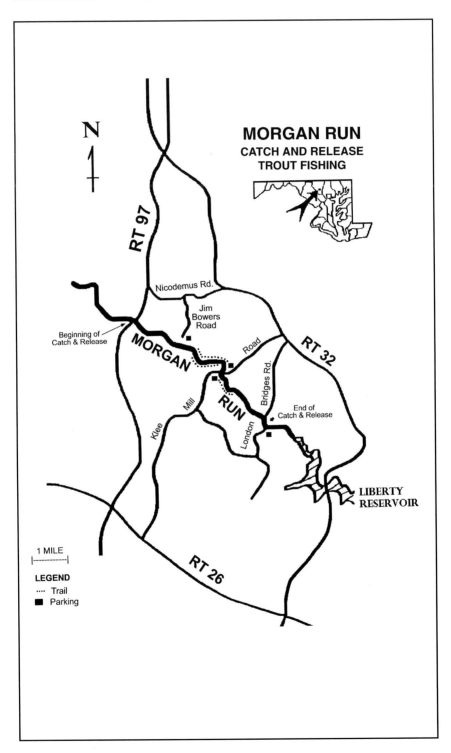

about every likely spot — anywhere where there is reasonable food, cover, and oxygen, and even in some places where there isn't.

Another plus for the stream is that there is a high density of fish. Usually between 2500 and 3000 trout are stocked annually over this small stretch. There is very limited reproduction on Morgan Run, and the reproduction that does occur is of brown trout. The holdover rate, when the summers are not too hot, can be quite good for the browns, better than the 30% figure we gave for the Patuxent. The rainbows do not hold as well, but given that the browns do well in this stream, the numbers of fish in the catch-and-release stretch can be quite high throughout the year.

Although naturally the fishing isn't always highly productive on Morgan Run, more than on most streams, it seems like the angler can almost always count on at least some action.

From late March through June is prime time on Morgan Run. Typical Maryland heat waves and droughts in the summer make fishing during these months more difficult, although still good. Fall can also be a great time on this stream, especially when there is some fall stocking, as occurs at times.

Shortly after March stocking, fishing a range of streamers is the ticket, but as soon as some mayflies and caddis appear, usually in later March and early April, nymph and dry fly fishing on Morgan Run becomes super. The fish often feed eagerly, and although they can be fussy at times, they rarely are highly selective. Those near the main access points become the most difficult to catch (and for some anglers, the most interesting) after they have experienced the sting of being caught several times. Often in those sections, fine tippets and smaller and more realistic patterns are required.

One of the reasons that Morgan Run can be such fun to fish is its openness. Even though the stream gets narrow in certain places, there is much more room to cast than, for example, the Patuxent River. Fly rods of any length are fine, although we tend to prefer those in the 7-8' range, with line weights from 2-6.

When fishing Morgan Run, hip boots are sufficient. Good polarized lenses also help, since this is a stream in which spotting the fish is both possible and very useful. For example, fish are at times podded up in certain fairly deep holes. It helps a great deal to be able to spot these fish, especially when running a small nymph through the hole. You can see just where the fish are, and often actually see the fish take.

Hatches, Other Stream Life, and Effective Patterns

Like its sister stream, the Patuxent River, Morgan Run does not have major hatches; but there is enough hatching to keep the fish active and alerted. There is the tiny black winter stonefly (#18) hatch in the first few months of the year, as well as some hatching of the larger brown stonefly (#14-16) that overlaps with the smaller black stonefly hatch, and continues into April. Some blue quills (#16-18) hatch throughout April, and blue-winged olives begin hatching about the same time (#16-20) and continue sporadically for many months. Look for them especially on cloudy and rainy days. Light cahills and some sulphurs (#14-16) appear in May. Caddisflies (#14-18) begin also in April and continue through fall. They come in a range of colors — black caddis (#18), olive-bodied caddis, tan caddis, and some cinnamon caddis with heavily mottled wings (all #14-16). Midges in a range of colors (#20-24) are abundant in this stream, and they are especially evident on the slow, deep pools.

Morgan Run is a particularly good terrestrial stream in the summer, and there is lots of aquatic life on this river. Look carefully and you will see many crayfish, as well as minnows, dace, and sculpins. These all make for fine fish taking patterns.

Regarding patterns, our experience in guiding and fishing on Morgan Run for many years is that the angler can do very well on it with a fairly small range of patterns. The Adams is a great mayfly imitation, and it is especially potent on Morgan Run in #14-18; Light Cahills (#14-16) are extremely effective beginning in May; and the Elk Hair Caddis, with bleached wings and olive or tan body (#14-18), is a dynamite pattern from April through fall. More than on the Patuxent, Morgan Run is also a good stream for nymphing, and the usual nymphs will take fish. Gold-Ribbed Hare's Ears, Pheasant Tails, and assortment of bead head nymphs, and caddis larva all are effective. Tan and olive are great colors.

Regarding terrestrials, although patterns for all major terrestrials work well on Morgan Run, we have found that the Black Ant, sizes #16-20, is consistently an exceptional fly. Try any specific pattern you want, but the traditional fur ant works as well as any. There are few things in life or fly fishing as pleasing as seeing sometimes fussy trout gently but decisively inhaling ants — and doing it often. As soon as the temperatures warm, especially from early June through summer and fall, Morgan Run can be an ant angler's nirvana.

We have noted that streamer fishing is especially potent in the colder months after the late winter stocking. Muddler Minnows (tan, #6-10), Clouser Minnows (tan/white and chartreuse/white, #6-10), and sculpin patterns (black and brown, #6-10) are all effective. But the two most effective flies during these months are the Patuxent Special and Woolly Bugger (see Chapter 13). When fished actively with quick one foot strips, the Patuxent Special, created by master fly tyer and angler Jay Sheppard of Laurel, Maryland, roughly imitates a tiny crayfish darting through the water. It may be the single most effective subsurface pattern that we have ever fished.

The Woolly Bugger is also effective in a wide range of color schemes. Larry has been particularly successful with what has been labeled the "neon woolly bugger." A story about this might be worth telling. A few years ago, Larry took Angus Phillips, noted outdoor editor for the Washington Post, to Morgan Run to try his hand at fly fishing for trout. For those of you who know Angus, you know he can be quite a disbeliever. So many fisherman have told him so many tall tales, that he half expects such tales — and doesn't expect that the fishing will be nearly as good as he is led to believe. Aware of this, and aware that Angus can be, shall we say, a bit pointed when he writes about an experience in the Post, Larry felt somewhat anxious as he took Angus to Morgan Run on a cold March day. Nothing

One of the gateways to Morgan Run.

could be seen hatching, and it was unlikely that any insect would appear even near the water. Early morning was totally dead. About 9 AM, when the water started warming a bit, the fish turned on dramatically to guess what? Woolly Buggers, #10, that Larry likes to tie with fluorescent red, chartreuse, and orange bodies. Angus termed the fly the Neon Woolly Bugger in happily reporting his experience in his Post column.

There is another "hatch" we should note on Morgan Run: the red worm hatch. Charlie vividly recalls a fishing outing he led to Morgan Run for the Potomac-Patuxent Chapter of Trout Unlimited on April Fool's Day some seasons ago. A light rain began falling as the anglers approached the stream at about 7:30 AM, and this rain continued, heavier at times, throughout the morning. Woolly Buggers and Patuxent Specials drew only short strikes. Charlie, who had rarely fished San Juan worm patterns previously, decided to tie a red one on. In the next three hours, he landed over 20 fish, and missed nearly as many more, while fishing only part of the time. When the group of 10 anglers met for lunch, after fishing in small groups in the morning, the results of the morning fishing were most interesting. All anglers who had used the red San Juan pattern caught many fish, including an 18" rainbow, while those who did not use the San Juan, caught few if any fish. The fish, in other words, had become highly selective to worm patterns! In line with this, our impression is that the San Juan is most effective on rainy days, when the stream bottom gets churned up and the "naturals" are more apparent in the water.

Finally, midge patterns, #20-24, are excellent fish takers, especially in the long, slow pools, for example, around the bridge at Klees Mill Road (see discussion of access points). Try both adult and subsurface patterns. Like in most midging situations, the Griffith's Gnat has been a top producer on Morgan Run when midges are fluttering on the water. (See Chapter 13 for our favorite midge patterns.)

The River and Its Problems

What does Morgan Run have to recommend it? As we have noted, you can fish in pretty surroundings and fish for trout that are often eager to feed. And there are lots of fish, perhaps a greater density of fish than in any stream in Maryland. The stream is open, so casting is generally easy. The river is close to Baltimore and not too far from Washington, D.C. And Morgan Run is accessible. Speaking of access, this is the only stream in the state that has a handicapped access area in the form of a ramp and a deck. This was effectively promoted by Frank Ryan, who is a Park Ranger for the DNR, and activist Art Nierenberg. Located above the bridge at Klees Mill Road, the deck was built by the Patapsco Valley Chapter of Trout Unlimited. Efforts such as this are needed on other Maryland streams.

Morgan Run does have some problems. The lack of a canopy of trees, while making the fishing easier, allows the stream to warm too much during summer heat waves. Trout have a hard time surviving, but in good summers a number of them do survive. Minimal reproduction is another of the stream's problems, and we can only speculate about why reproduction isn't greater on a river that seems to have all the right habitat. Water warming is likely a factor, as is sediment deposited in the stream from farms above the catch-and-release area. The state now owns some of the land above the special area, and has improved the habitat. Further habitat improvement would be a boon to Morgan Run.

Poaching was at one time a large-scale problem on Morgan Run. However, thanks to the yeoman efforts of Ranger Frank Ryan, this problem has diminished in recent years. According to Frank, fish taking is still a big problem, and if this problem could be solved, reproduction would increase substantially. As of this writing Frank no longer patrols Morgan Run. Many believe Frank's vigilant patrolling saved Morgan Run. He set a standard for future rangers, and we can only hope that "unauthorized activity" continues to be kept at bay on this stream, and others as well.

Location and Access Points: How To Get There

As noted, the Morgan Run Special Area is located in Carroll County. It begins where Route 97 crosses the stream and ends at London Bridges Road about three miles downstream. There are three access points with parking areas: Jim Bowers Road for the upper section, Klees Mill Road for the middle section, and London Bridges Road for the lower section. To get to Jim Bowers Road, you go

Another fine pool on Morgan Run.

north on Route 97 to about a mile after this highway crosses the stream. Turn right onto Nicodemus Road, and after another mile, make a sharp right onto Jim Bowers Road. The dirt road that will take you to the stream will be apparent to you. Park in the parking area at the end of Jim Bowers Road. The other two access points are straightforward. See the map that is provided.

One point worth noting is that much of this stream has no clearcut paths. You have to work your way through the woods, being careful to avoid pricker bushes. There are some paths, for example, on both sides of the stream going downstream from Klees Mill Road for about 200 hundred yards.

Generally the upper parts of Morgan Run are smaller waters, although you will still have some casting room. Fish will be throughout the three mile catch-and-release stretch. The Klees Mill section is probably the most popular. This is

Small waters in the upper section of Morgan Run.

where the handicapped access has been created, and there are plenty of fish within a hundred yards upstream or downstream of the bridge. Upstream from the bridge is probably the most picturesque part of the stream, as you will encounter large boulders, fast chutes and plenty of pocket water, with some deep pools interspersed. At this point, Morgan Run seems like a different river from the rest of its reaches. But wherever you fish this little gem, there will be plenty of trout and an abundance of beauty.

CHAPTER 3
THE PATUXENT RIVER

A Trout River Close to Two Cities

T he catch-and-release section of the Patuxent River is about a 12-mile stretch of water within an hour's drive of both Baltimore and Washington, D. C. We consider this little river our home water, and have fished on it since each of us began fly fishing. The Patuxent is also one of our favorite rivers on which to guide. There is much beauty in this river system, and trout, too. Although it is not without its problems, the Patuxent can be an exceptionally productive trout fishery.

Flowing from springs near the town of Damascus (west of Route 27), the Patuxent becomes a fishable piece of water near where Long Corner Road crosses it, and contains fish throughout the 12 mile catch-and-release stretch. This special section ends at Route 97, and the River flows into Triadelphia Reservoir shortly beyond that point. The stream is located within the Patuxent River State Park, and is the dividing line between Howard and Montgomery Counties.

Throughout its reaches, the Patuxent is a low gradient stream that winds slowly through wooded areas and a few meadows. One of the enticing features of this river is that, although it is close to heavily populated areas, when fishing it, one can easily get a sense of being away from it all — of being out in the woods, often with no one around. In fact, as you walk to some of the "backwoods" sections, on some of the 3000 acres of state-owned land surrounding the Patuxent, you can get a sense of being very far away. The woods abound with wildlife. If you look closely, during even a single day outing, you may see wood duck, beaver, woodcock, and perhaps a great blue heron or two.

The Patuxent usually ranges from about 15 to 40 feet wide. It is mostly a gravel bottom river, with some sections that are rocky and others that are clay bottomed. Throughout its many twists and turns, the angler will see numerous undercut banks, fallen trees, and root systems, all of which harbor trout during most of the year, including some true trophy fish. The angler will also encounter some riffles, runs, and chutes. You will spot lots of deep holes, although not many exceed five feet or so.

There is a fine canopy of trees over the Patuxent. These trees serve to shade the river nicely, so that even in the dead of a Maryland summer, the temperature rarely exceeds about 72 degrees at the hottest point of the day. The water temperatures cool considerably during evenings. Also, the Patuxent has several little feeder streams that provide cooling during the summer doldrums. Check your maps for these feeders, and fish below them when water temps rise. Trout seek out those cooler waters.

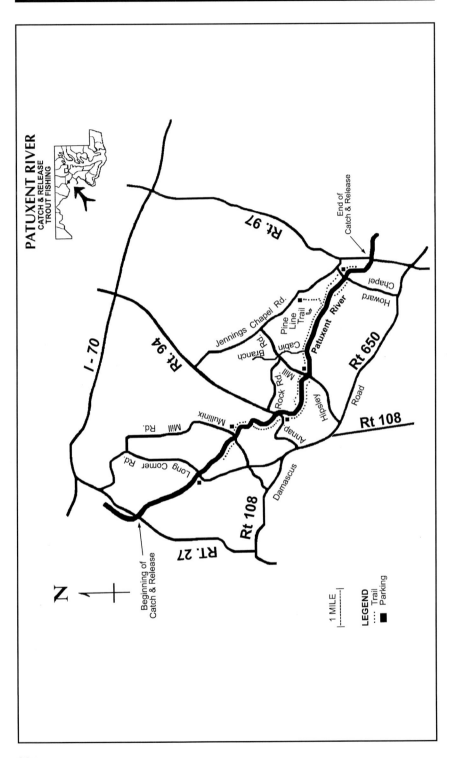

PATUXENT RIVER
CATCH & RELEASE
TROUT FISHING

End of Catch & Release

Rt. 97

Chapel
Howard

Jennings Chapel Rd.

Pine Line Trail

Patuxent River

Cabin Branch Rd.

Rt. 94

I-70

Rt 650

Mill Rd.

Rock Rd.

Hipsley

Annap

Rt 108

Mullinix

Mill Rd.

Long Corner Rd.

Damascus

Rt 108

Rt. 27

N

Beginning of
Catch & Release

1 MILE

LEGEND
······ Trail
■ Parking

The most fishable tributary to the Patuxent is the little Cabin Branch. This stream, like the main stem, contains some reproduction of brown trout and a good holdover of stocked browns. It is also stocked with rainbows. But beware! This is tiny water, often 10- to 15-feet wide, and it is surrounded by lots of brush, including more pricker bushes than at times seem imaginable. Take a small rod to the Cabin Branch (we like to use 6-1/2 to 7' fly rods there). There are some large browns in this tributary.

As you explore the Patuxent, you will encounter varied terrain. On one side of the river you may notice tall reed grass, while on the other there will be steep hills lined with a variety of trees. In fact, there are some huge trees along the banks of this little stream, and these provide both shading and beauty. You will see oaks, sycamores, maples, and beech trees. Jay Sheppard of the Potomac-Patuxent Chapter of Trout Unlimited organized efforts to plant and then prune over 300 small sycamores in the late 1980s. Jay is a master fly fisherman and guide, who is considered by Patuxent anglers to be the dean of this river. He has named many of the pools on the river, and it is said that he knows many of the fish by name. In any event, many of the sycamores that Jay and his buddies planted have survived to grow up, and now serve to firm up banks and provide much needed shade in the dog days of summer.

The other type of vegetation you will encounter on the Patuxent, as on the Cabin Branch noted above, is the *Rosa multiflora* — the dreaded pricker bush. These are the bane of the trout angler's existence, as well as the salvation of the salmonids inhabiting the river. They provide cover for the fish, and they have eaten more of our flies than we care to remember. They will also do grave harm to your waders if you don't avoid them. Charlie vividly recalls a day many seasons ago when he first began fishing the Patuxent. He was the proud owner of a new pair of his first felt soled hip boots — what then seemed like very expensive ones. By the end of a day of tangling with thorns, the boots were not a pretty sight. Multiflora are to be avoided, at all costs!

The Fish and the Fishing

As we have mentioned, the catch-and-release stretch contains mostly brown trout and rainbows. The brownies have been reproducing for some years now, and there is a decent holdover rate of stocked browns, depending of course on the weather conditions in summer and winter. In some years, the holdover of stocked browns has been reported to be over 30% (a good figure when you consider that holdovers accumulate over years), whereas in the worst of years, when summer droughts seem to dry everything up, holdover is low. Thankfully, the streambred fish seem to survive regardless of the weather conditions.

There is little if any reproduction of rainbows, and in most years, the angler will see few bows after about the middle of July. On other years, some rainbows do hold over and seem healthy and feisty throughout the year. In the spring of 1995, as an experiment, the Department of Natural Resources stocked a few hundred cutthroat trout in the Patuxent and other Maryland waters. Fall shocking found no trace of these westerners, however, and our expectation is that further stocking of cuts will not occur.

One exciting feature of the Patuxent Special Area is that chance for a big brown. There are a few Maryland streams that harbor the biggest fish, and we believe the Patuxent is one of them. Although they are rare, there always is the sense that a five pounder is possible. Each year there are reports of a few fish that are over 20 inches caught and released in these waters and there have been reports (even some reliable ones!) of fish in the 24 to 26" range being taken. Each of us has landed fish in the 20" range and seen others that were bigger. These fish are rarely if ever taken on a dry fly. They behave like most big browns, hovering under root systems, in deep holes, and in undercut banks. Your best chance of spotting the submarines is autumn, when the spawning urge brings the biggest fish onto their redds. Whether or not you choose to fish to spawners, it is fascinating to observe these bruisers performing their spawning ritual.

Stocking policies on the Patuxent have been wise, and have taken into account what the river is able to support, as well as the wild trout population. Each year, about 3000-4000 browns and rainbows are stocked, with the browns being float stocked throughout much of the catch-and-release area. This float stocking is conducted by the Potomac-Patuxent Chapter of TU, and it has been annually organized and led for many consecutive years by Sheppard.

More than perhaps any river we have fished, the Patuxent can be either feast or famine. On some days, catching fish there can be incredibly easy — a guide's dream. On other days, it would take a combination of Vincent Marinaro, Ed Shenck, and Joan Wulff herself to land anything other than a nine-inch fallfish. Fortunately, though, there have not been too many days like the latter.

There is a common misunderstanding that we have noticed among anglers who are not regulars on this river. We often hear that the Patuxent is not a good river for surface fishing. Our experience is quite different. Although there are no prolific hatches on the Patuxent, and despite the fact that we have fished when no fish could be seen rising throughout an entire hatch, we have experienced very good dry fly fishing. Trout will mysteriously turn off the surface at times. But they are rarely selective, and when they feed on the surface, a range of imitations and attractors will work. Pete Yarrington, a talented local angler and fly tyer, tells the story of a fisherman several years ago who he observed landing nine rainbows on nine consecutive casts, all while fishing a slow, clear pool with a royal coachman! We hasten to add, though, that the dry fly fishing is best when something is indeed hatching. The fish may not be selective on the Patuxent, but hatches do help to get trout activated and pointed to the surface.

Despite the fine dry fly fishing, it is true that Patuxent is at its best for subsurface fishing, particularly streamer fishing. This is the home of the Patuxent Special, one of the best all around subsurface patterns around. It should not surprise you by now that this fly was created by Jay Sheppard. Jay, like most of us who fish it a lot, believe that when stripped quickly though the water, the Patuxent Special (see Chapter 13) imitates a tiny, darting crayfish. Other streamer patterns

Log jams, overhangs and narrowness reflect the complex nature of the Patuxent River.

that work well on the Patuxent will be noted in the next section of fly patterns. When fishing streamer-type patterns, look for the likely spots — the undercut banks, root systems, fallen trees, deep holes — and keep the fly moving. And be prepared; you never know what lurks in the shadows of the Patuxent.

The good cover above and around the Patuxent has a downside. It seems that there is always a pricker bush, an overhang, or a nearby tree waiting to gobble up your fly or lure. Our advise to anglers, particularly fly anglers because of the kind of rods they use and the casting that is required, is to take notice of what is around you before every cast, and work actively to avoid hook ups with anything other than fish. It is generally best to use a short line, and roll casting can be a great advantage, if not necessary. Side casts also can help.

Tackle and equipment should fit the requirements of a small, brushy stream with some deep holes. We like short fly rods, anywhere from about 6-1/2 to 8 feet, for 2 to 6 weight lines, depending on what kinds of flies you are using. Although there are some advantages to longer rods (e.g., you can reach further to dap your fly), most fly rodders believe the quarters are just too tight for them.

You can get by on a lot of this stream with hip boots, but there are sections that require chest waders, e.g, the section above Howard Chapel Road (see access points). The chest waders give you just that many more degrees of freedom when fishing other deep holes on the river.

Hatches, Other Stream life, and Effective Patterns

Although there are no spectacular hatches on the Patuxent, there is a wide range of insects hatching. The years starts with good hatches of tiny black winter stoneflies (about #18), which lasts into March; larger (#14-16) brown stoneflies also occur in later winter and early spring. On sunny winter days, you can find fish rising to these stones (as well as a variety of midges). In April, blue quills (#16-20) hatch, as well as black caddisflies (#18-20). Also, a tan caddis appears in April (#14-16). In fact, the river will see a variety of caddis hatches from spring into the fall season.

In May, sulphurs (#14-18) and light cahills (#14) hatch in fair numbers, and trout often will feed eagerly on them. On the Patuxent, though, we have observed the curious phenomenon during sulphur season of good hatching occurring without any rising fish. During these times, we have often had the day saved by using sulphur wet fly patterns such as the Little Marryat (see Chapter 13).

June will witness an isonychia (#8-12) hatch, which appears again in September. Other than the isonychia, there are not significant mayfly hatches in summer. However, there are caddisflies hatching occasionally during summer, and on cloudy days throughout much of the year, blue-winged olives (#18) tend to hatch.

As we mentioned, Patuxent trout tend not to be selective. When they do rise, usually a range of flies will take them. At the same time, using patterns that at least approximate what is hatching is a good idea. Patterns of the same names as the flies noted above are effective during hatch times. For caddisflies, Elk Hair Caddis work well, although it is wise to try something more realistic in the slower pools. A Henryville Special often does the trick. Also, an appropriately sized Adams works well for a number of hatches, as well as in non-hatch situations. For example, an #18 Adams is a fine fish taker during spring hatches on blue quills, during blue-winged olive hatches, and even during black winter stonefly hatches. On the other hand, a #12 Adams takes fish well when the isonychia hatches in June and September.

Nymphs, wet flies, and caddis larva and pupa are naturally effective in the sizes that fit the naturals and imitations we have noted above. Go to them when the dry fly action is off (or of course if you prefer nymphing).

During summer, terrestrials are the ticket. Ants, Beetles, and Hoppers in a range of sizes work very well, especially in slower pools and along the banks. We have been surprised that large Ants (e.g., #14) are often highly effective on the Patuxent. In the fall, these patterns continue to work, but Crickets (#10) also become dynamite patterns. Listen to the sounds of fall, and when you start hearing crickets sing their song, shift to a black cricket pattern. The fish are usually eager.

As far as aquatic life, this stream is loaded with it. Crayfish abound, and are a favorite of the trout. Dace and minnows are very common, and the trout love them. Regarding subsurface patterns, we have already mentioned the Patuxent Special as a rough crayfish imitation (see Chapter 13). Other patterns that take fish

Jay Sheppard landing a trout on the Patuxent.

very well are the Muddler Minnow, Woolly Buggers, Clouser Minnows, and Sculpins. Sizes #6 to 10 are effective.

The River and Its Problems

We have already talked about the Patuxent's glories: It has a beauty all its own, an eerie beauty that is in places reminiscent of a bayou as much as a trout stream; one can find solitude and serenity on this river, and there is a sense of being away from it all; there are wild fish here as well as stocked fish; and there is always the chance of hooking into a very large fish.

The Patuxent is not without its problems, though. Although the water stays cool, the flow gets very low in summer, and in drought years it can get terribly low. At times it seems like the river is not moving at all. Because of the stress that low flow (and thus low oxygen) causes the fish, we find ourselves staying away from the river in the dog days of July and August. If you fish during those times, early morning is a must — from dawn to about 10 AM, or possibly the last hour or two of daylight. Land and release your fish quickly.

The river also has a lot of silt, which creates problems for both insect life and fish. We always look forward to heavy winter and early spring rains that flush a lot of the silt out of the river.

By far the biggest problem faced by the Patuxent and its fish is that of poaching. Since there are several miles of back woods, it is impossible for the State of Maryland to provide all the resources needed to "cover" this river. And we have run into some pretty scary characters poaching on the Patuxent. Rather than confront poachers when you have a sense that this would be unsafe, we suggest that you call Department of Natural Resources Catch-a-Poacher (1-800-635-6124) or the Maryland State Parks and Forests Dispatcher number (1-800-825-PARK). To the extent that you can, try to provide time, date, location, description, license number and the like. Although going through the trouble is a hassle, this lovely river is worth protecting.

Location and Access Points: How to Get There

The Patuxent River Special Area borders Howard and Montgomery County, and runs parallel to Route 650, Old Damascus Road. The upstream section of the catch-and-release stretch is where Route 27 crosses the river and runs for about 12 miles downstream to where Route 97 crosses it. There are five major access points to the river, as you can see from the map. The best fishing is from Route 97 upstream to where Long Corner Road crosses the river.

Each section of the river fishes a little different, and each has somewhat different features. As noted earlier, for example, the section upstream from Howard Chapel Road requires chest waders. The section above Mullinix Mill Road is small water, often only about 10' wide, and contains mostly wild browns and hold-overs. The section around Long Corner Road has nearly all wild fish. The middle section is most heavily stocked. From Mullinix Mill Road down to Route 97, each section has its share of deep pools, some running for as much as 100 yards. These tend to be great places for dry fly fishing.

Bridle paths run on one side of the river or the other throughout most of its reaches, but there are sections without any paths. For example, from where Howard Chapel Road crosses, upstream for several miles, there are no clear paths. When walking back to your car, it is best either to walk the river back, or stay close to the river as you walk the banks. There is a catch to this prescription, however, because if you get very close to the river you encounter heavy thickets of pricker bushes that can tangle you to a halt. Our map provides dotted lines demarcating some of the main paths. Note that if you walk the banks, it is best not to leave the flood plain. Things can get pretty confusing if you do, and although we haven't lost any anglers in this way, wandering through the woods can be anxiety provoking, and can ruin a good day.

CHAPTER 4
THE MIDDLE PATUXENT
Far Away in Suburbia

T he delayed harvest section of the Middle Patuxent River is even closer to suburban life than the main Patuxent. Yet because it is embedded in Howard County park land, the angler is able to experience a sense of being away from it all, like on the main Patuxent, and partake of the serenity that is such a prized part of the trout fishing experience. The Middle Patuxent twists and turns over two and one-half to three miles of special regulation water. As the angler fishes upstream or downstream, each new turn seems to offer an interesting piece of structure for trout.

This section of the Middle Patuxent is the most recent special regulation trout water in the state. The delayed harvest policy went into effect in January 1999. From October 1 until June 15, all fish must be released, and only artificial flies and lures are permitted. From June 16 through September 30, the angler can harvest two trout per day, and there are no tackle restrictions. Thus, there are plenty of trout in the delayed harvest section from fall to early summer, beyond which point the warming water and reduced flows make it harder for trout, especially rainbows, to survive.

This section of the Middle Patuxent has been near and dear to us. Larry was instrumental in the opening up of the section to trout fishing, and Charlie is the Middle Patuxent chairman of the Potomac-Patuxent Chapter of Trout Unlimited. Larry had known and fished for smallmouth bass in these waters for years. When it became clear that the state's Department of Natural Resources was receptive to ideas for new trout fishing opportunities, Larry studied the entire section, with an eye toward suitable trout habitat, insect life, and accessibility. Given the potential that he believed this section to have, Larry contacted the DNR's Director of Coldwater Fisheries, Bob Lunsford. Bob is always on the lookout for fishing possibilities, and after examining the section, agreed that a delayed harvest regulation made the best sense.

The Middle Patuxent River originates from springs many miles upstream, and has a number of small feeders entering it throughout its course. The delayed harvest section also has several small feeders that enhance flow and cool temperatures. As we have noted, this section has numerous twists and turns, and it seems like each turn creates good structure, where the water runs against one of the banks, against boulders, and deepens.

Even though much of this stretch is surrounded by housing developments, these are enough of a distance from the river that houses are rarely visible to the

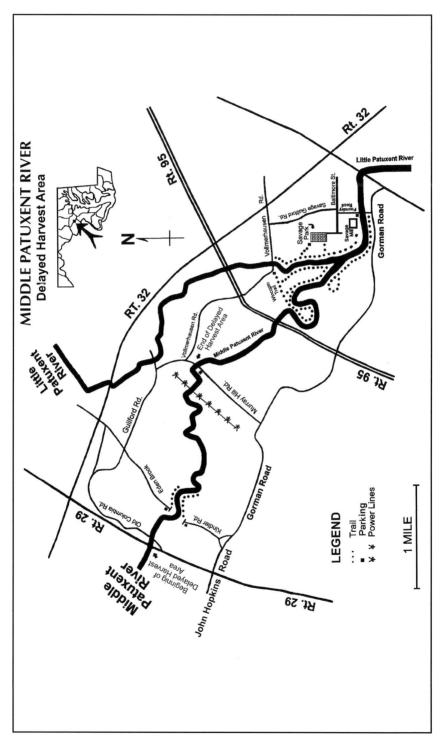

MIDDLE PATUXENT RIVER
Delayed Harvest Area

N

LEGEND

··· Trail
■ Parking
⁂ Power Lines

1 MILE

angler. Instead, what the angler sees are steep hills and low bottoms, heavily wooded by a variety of hardwoods and hemlocks, and spotted with laurel. Banks adjoining the river tend to be steep, but not too steep to be climbed by most anglers.

The stream itself ranges from about 25 to 50' in width, and is well canopied with trees throughout. The river bottom exhibits a lot of variety. There are rocky sections with large boulders, spots with rock table, portions with considerable gravel, and some sandy spots. This variety is also reflected in the water. Much of the delayed harvest section is low gradient, as it winds through the woods, but there are also rocky-bottomed, semi-swift rapids.

As of this writing, a beaver dam exists in the lower third of the delayed harvest section. This dam has created a deep pool that is probably 100' long and 50' wide. Also, the dam has backed up and deepened the river for about a quarter of a mile upstream. This is a nice holding area for trout. Of course, beaver dams such as this come and go; they could last for several seasons, or get blown out tomorrow in one big gully washer. There are several log jams created by fallen trees that create good cover for trout.

The Fish and the Fishing

The special area is stocked in spring and fall. The fall stocking occurs after October 1, when the catch-and-release policy has again kicked in and flows have increased. The Potomac-Patuxent Chapter of TU float stocks the entire delayed harvest stretch. Thus, fish are distributed nicely throughout. Rainbows and brown trout are stocked here, with most in the 10-14" range, although occasional submarines are found in this water. Some holdover, especially of brown trout, occurs from one year to the next, and these holdover trout can be considerably larger. At this point, it is not clear just what the holdover capability of this stretch is. We can note, though, that on a February day, after one of the worst late summer and fall droughts in recorded history, we saw a good number of trout. Thus, there is some degree of holdover of trout from the fall stocking into spring, and even some from one spring to the next.

Since the Middle Patuxent had been stocked for two seasons prior to special regulations, we have spent some hours studying and fishing this water. Fishing can be fine on the surface or below, although at this point we have mostly fished streamers and nymph patterns, with considerable success. Whatever pattern you use, it is important to understand that this river seems to alternate between stretches of flat, fairly shallow water that holds few fish, and sections that have trout, trout, trout written all over them. The latter usually occur at points where the river twists and turns, as we have noted. They are marked by runs that empty into deeper pools with great rock structure.

In fishing the Middle Patuxent, you can use fly rods of any length, from 6' to 9'. The shorter rods are easier to maneuver, whereas the longer rods facilitate roll casting, which is an advantage on a stream that has high banks lined with trees. At the same time, if the angler casts upstream, there is plenty of room on this stream for long casting, when that is necessary.

Regarding leaders and tippets, either 7-1/2 or 9' leaders are fine, and 4X or 5X tippets also are suitable. However, prescriptions such as this can be hazardous. Our impression at this early date is that this section, like the upper Patuxent, has good midge hatching, as well as smaller mayflies (see next section on hatching). When using smaller size flies, the angler should shift to 6X tippet, or perhaps even 7X in low summer flows.

Although hip boots are fine during summer flows, we recommend chest waders during higher flows, especially in spring. Felt soles are a very good idea because you will encounter plenty of slippery rocks. When wading, watch out for very sandy spots. At times it will seem like the bottom is sliding out from under you. This is not a dangerous situation, but does warrant slow, careful wading if you don't want to get wet!

Hatches, Other Stream Life, and Effective Patterns

Although we have observed plenty of insect life on the Middle Patuxent, not a lot is yet known about its hatches. We expect them to be very similar to hatching on the upper Patuxent, but more study is needed before we can comment confidently.

What we have observed are tiny black winter stoneflies (#18) and brown stoneflies (#14-16) during winter months, a variety and good number of caddis flies, midges, and several different mayflies (blue-winged olives, light cahills). Terrestrials do provide excellent fishing in summer and fall: ants, beetles, crickets, inchworms.

A range of nymphs will take fish on the Middle Patuxent, with the old standbys working as well as anything: Gold-Ribbed Hare's Ears, assorted bead head patterns, Pheasant Tails, and caddis larva and pupa, (all in the #14-18 range). Especially on rainy days or when the water is a bit off color, try red San Juan worms (#14). This fine fish taker can become even better when rainy conditions kick up worms in the water.

As with the upper Patuxent, the Middle Patuxent is rich with baitfish. There is a great supply of dace, chubs, fallfish, sculpins, and crayfish. That is why assorted streamer patterns, Woolly Buggers, and Sheppard's Patuxent Specials work so well on this river (see discussion of Patuxent Special in last chapter on the upper Patuxent; see also fly pattern recipe in Chapter 13).

The River and Its Problems

The delayed harvest section of the Middle Patuxent is only 15 minutes from the Washington beltway, less than a half hour from the Baltimore beltway, and just down the hill from housing developments. Yet, this is a river that creates a very

The Middle Patuxent showing its own monuments.

distinct sense of being away from it all, and it holds a good supply of trout for most of the year.

Although more data are needed, we suspect the main problem of this river is low and warming water in summer. Based on our observations, it is likely that some holdover from one year to the next will occur, especially of brown trout, but we doubt that the numbers will be great. In addition, due to the lack of spawning habitat, we would expect very limited natural reproduction of trout. Because of these problems, the Middle Patuxent is a natural for Maryland's delayed harvest program.

Another problem is rather limited access. There are only two main access points — the upper and lowermost parts of the delayed harvest section; and only in the lower section is the parking area very close to the fishing. There is of course a great up side to this: The angler gets to have a nice walk to the river, and has greater solitude when he or she gets there.

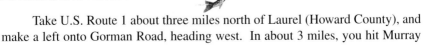

Location and Access Points

Take U.S. Route 1 about three miles north of Laurel (Howard County), and make a left onto Gorman Road, heading west. In about 3 miles, you hit Murray

Fallen trees and bordering hemlocks give the Middle Patuxent a far away feel.

Hill Road. If you take a right there, you will cross the stream in about a mile. Park at the stream and fish upstream, as the downstream side is posted property. If you continue on Gorman Road, it will veer right in about a mile, and run into Kindler Road. Take Kindler Road to a dead end. Park there, and walk down to the stream. You can fish from that point, downstream. There is a path on your right, but that will run out in about a quarter of a mile.

From Route 29, you can get to Kindler Road by taking a right on Johns Hopkins Road (about three miles north of Burtonsville), and then a left onto Gorman Road, and another quick left onto Kindler Road.

Finally, you can also approach the stream from its north side by going east on Route 32 off Route 29, or west on 32 off Route 95. Take the Eden Brook Road off 32. Follow the Eden Brook Road signs; this road dead ends in a parking area, and it is a short walk to the river.

The Savage Mill Section

Although our emphasis is on the streams with catch-and-release policies, we would be remiss if we did not add a few words about another section of the Middle Patuxent River and its sister river, the Little Patuxent. These sections offer fine fishing possibilities, similar in quality to the delayed harvest section. And the fish

The Falls – a scenic section above the Old Savage Mill.

hold over well into summer. Virtually all of what we have said about fishing tactics and tackle on the delayed harvest section apply to these waters. Our impression, though, is that larger fish are stocked in these sections.

About a mile or so downstream of where the delayed harvest section of the Middle Patuxent ends, the river runs under Interstate 95. From this point to where the Middle Patuxent joins with the Little Patuxent, the river is stocked, mostly with rainbow trout, and there is a two fish limit. There are no tackle restrictions here.

The Little Patuxent River, too, is stocked from Vollmerhausen Road to where it joins the Middle Patuxent. Although the Little is a somewhat smaller river than the Middle, it is similar in habitat and in fishing potential. It also has a two fish limit with no bait restrictions.

When the Middle and Little Patuxent Rivers join, they become the Little Patuxent (thus forming something of a linguistic nightmare!). We call this the Savage Mill section. At this point, the river acquires a very different character. It possesses a steeper gradient, faster water, and resembles a brawling, boulder strewn western river more than the Piedmont region stream that it is. The same fishing regulations apply to this section as to those just noted, but the angler has the opportunity for another kind of fishing experience, given the structure of this section. This section is usually stocked in the fall as well as the spring.

To get to the Savage Mill section, you take Route 1 north to Gorman Road. Turn left on Gorman Road, and within a mile you hit Foundry Road. The river is a few yards from that point, and there is ample parking at the bridge. A path follows the river on the left side through much of this section.

CHAPTER 5
THE PAINT BRANCH
A Stream Worth Saving

I t was a mild October afternoon, and Charlie had a couple of hours to kill. He decided to spend the time fishing the little Paint Branch, which was about 15 minutes from home. Some autumn rains had produced a good flow on this tiny Piedmont stream, and the colors of autumn made things look about as good as one could imagine. In a couple of hours, five wild brown trout, all between 9 and 12 inches, were caught and released. Each fell for a simple #16 Elk Hair Caddis. The fishing experience felt as good to the angler as most days involving many more fish and much bigger fish.

The above is what the Paint Branch is capable of yielding. It is the kind of stream one can enjoyably fish for a few hours. You don't go there to "bang fish." Instead, you go to enjoy a tiny stream that flows through lovely, wooded Maryland park land and is inhabited by wild brown trout. All of this occurs right smack in the middle of sprawling suburban life.

The Paint Branch is located in suburban Montgomery County, and the catch-and-release section covers a couple of miles from Fairland Road upstream to its headwaters. This is a classic small Piedmont stream, with undercut banks, nice root systems, fallen trees, and a combination of gravel and sand on the bottom. The Paint Branch is the smallest stream we include in this book, with the average width being between 10 and 20'.

The fact that the Paint Branch had a reproducing brown trout population was first discovered in 1974 by Chuck Woods, a local angler and TU leader. By 1980 a section of the stream was designated as catch-and-release, artificial lures and flies only. Studies done by the Department of Natural Resources indicate that as of this writing there have been 21 consecutive years of brown trout reproduction on the stream (no year class failures). The stream has not been stocked for many years, with the last record of brown trout stocking being in 1943.

The Potomac-Patuxent Chapter of Trout Unlimited (PPTU) has worked vigorously over the years to protect and enhance this fragile little jewel from the effects of development. TU leaders like Bob Schueler, Dick Blaylock, and now David Dunmire have devoted untold hours to stream protection and enhancement projects; and Maryland's Coldwater Fisheries personnel have been an important part of this work. In 1994, Dunmire was instrumental in creating the Eyes of the Paint Branch, an activist group that aims to produce public awareness and advocacy about the stream.

The Fish and the Fishing

As we have said, the Paint Branch is inhabited by streambred brown trout. It has not been stocked for many years. The trout are not large, with few being more than 12". Much of the reproduction occurs in tiny tributaries in the stream's upper reaches, although reproduction also occurs throughout the several miles of the stream. Only the section north of Fairland Road is designated as catch-and-release, but this is the kind of resource in which trout should be released wherever they are caught. The resource simply could not sustain itself if anglers did not release their catch.

The Paint Branch certainly does not have a density of fish found in the major rivers of Maryland. At the same time, one can find trout in just about all of the likely holding spots. As you walk the stream, the holding areas are pretty obvious, as are the areas that do not hold fish. Usually the latter are just too shallow for trout. Even in the midst of drought conditions, you will spot trout, although when the water is very low, these little critters are just about uncatchable.

If there ever was a stream that Mother Nature structured for the small rod, the Paint Branch is it. An ideal rod is in the 6 to 7-1/2' range, with suitable line weights in the 2-5 range. Hip boots rather than chest waders are best. Wear dull colors to avoid spooking trout, move very slowly, and be sure to have a good pair of polarized glasses. Be careful of the tendency to walk up to good holding spots. You can get away with that on most streams if you move slowly. On the Paint Branch, however, doing so will just about assure you that no fish will bend your rod. This is the kind of stream on which it is necessary to keep a low profile and stay a distance from the fish. Make medium length casts to prevent spooking these jittery browns. Nearly all your fishing should involve a careful, upstream approach. Occasionally, a down stream cast to a deeper hole is possible, provided that you do not get too close to the fish.

Dry fly fishing on the Paint Branch, in our experience, is preferred over nymphing. That is because it is easier to detect a strike on the surface when fishing from the distances we recommend, e.g., 30-40'. Also, there is a special thrill to seeing a trout whack a fly on the surface in a tiny stream. On the other hand, the close quarters make "tight line" nymphing difficult, since you could not get close enough to the fish to do this kind of angling. Nymphing with a strike indicator is possible, although not easy in a tiny stream such as this. Streamer fishing, on the other hand, can be quite effective, provided that it is done with some finesse and flows are good.

Hatches, Other Stream Life, and Effective Patterns

The first hatch to appear on the Paint Branch is the early brown stonefly, about #14. These appear in good numbers from January through March. They are followed by a yellow/brown stonefly (#12-14) in late January, and a little green stonefly (#14-16) from March through June.

The small size of the paint Branch calls for a stealthy approach.

Mayflies begin to appear in good numbers in April. The Paint Branch does get modest hatches of the "April grays" — the Henderickson (#12), blue quill (#18), and the quill gordon (#14). The March brown (#10-12) hatches from early May to late May. Blue-winged olives (#16-20) begin in May and can be seen on cloudy days through fall. The isonychia (#10) hatches in June.

Regarding caddisflies, the early green caddis (#12-14) will begin to show up in April, as well the little black sedge (#18). The cinnamon caddis, with mottled wings and a cinnamon brown body (#16), is present from about mid-June through September.

Most of these insects may be imitated with surface patterns of the same name. To these we would add the ever-effective Adams and the Three-Hackle, which is described in the pattern section (Chapter 13). When caddises are on the water, the Elk or Deer Hair Caddis is highly effective. Terrestrials are abundant on the Paint Branch, especially beetles (#16-18) and black ants (#16-20). Like so many wild trout that are not heavily fished over, the Paint Branch brownies are very spooky, but they are rarely selective. If you don't spook them, many different patterns will get their interest.

There is a good supply of baitfish on the Paint Branch. Dace, sculpins, and crayfish are all present. We especially like small Woolly Buggers (#10-12) and Patuxent Specials (#10, see pattern in Chapter 13).

The River and Its Problems

The Paint Branch is a tiny jewel that has been constantly threatened by local development. Although the PPTU, the Eyes of the Paint Branch, and DNR biologists have all worked in concert to protect the stream, it seems like the battle is never-ending. The proposed intercounty connector, a highway meant to connect Gaithersburg to Laurel, has been a threat for decades. PPTU and Eyes of the Paint Branch have effectively marshalled support against building the road, but the possibility seems to never go away. If the road is ever built, one has to wonder if the stream can survive as a viable wild trout fishery.

Similarly, if this little stream is to thrive, anglers who partake of its pleasures need to be ever-mindful of its fragile nature. Care must be taken to release fish properly and to not trample spawning beds.

Location and Access Points

The catch-and-release section of the Paint Branch can be reached from Route 29 in Montgomery County. Take Route 29 to Fairland Road, and go west on Fairland Road. Cross the stream and park on the south side of Fairland Road, close to the stream. The catch-and-release section is upstream from Fairland Road. This special regulation section can also be accessed from Briggs Chaney Road, which is also off Route 29, north of Fairland Road. You can fish the water below the catch-and-release section downstream from Fairland Road. It is best to walk downstream and then fish it back up. Fishing down will simply chase the fish away! Again, even when fishing the open water, it is advisable not to keep fish. Releasing your catch will help maintain a fragile wild trout resource that so many people have worked to protect and that is truly a treasure that is worth saving.

CHAPTER 6
BIG HUNTING CREEK
The Stream of Presidents

B ig Hunting Creek is a classic freestone mountain stream nestled in the Catoctin Mountains above the little town of Thurmont. The catch-and-release section covers about two and a half miles of choice water. Big Hunting Creek was the first Maryland stream to be designated as catch-and-release, and for many years the sole stream that was marked as fly fishing only. Most other catch-and-release streams still permit both artificial lures and flies.

Big Hunting has some neat fly fishing history associated with it. Located a stone's throw from Camp David, the mountain retreat of U.S. presidents, it was avidly fly fished by Presidents Eisenhower and Carter. In fact, one of the famed holes on the stream is called the President's Hole. There always seems to be a few huge fish in that hole. The stream is also home of the Brotherhood of the Jungle Cock, a group formed over 50 years ago and devoted to teaching youngsters to fly fish. The famous angler, Joe Brooks, helped form this group back in 1940, and the story goes that the idea was spawned one spring night when Joe and his fishing buddies were stranded in a cabin as a blizzard ruined their fishing trip. The Brotherhood continues, to this day, to fulfill its teaching mission. The Joe Brooks Memorial stands in the upper section of the special area as a tribute to the work this great angler did for Big Hunting Creek and for fishing in general.

Big Hunting Creek can be at once a very demanding and a very exciting stream to fish. Located in Frederick County, the Special Area of Big Hunting Creek begins with some tiny water above the dam at Cunningham Falls Lake. The main section, though, is from the dam downstream to a point just above Frank Bentz Pond. This stream has all of the features one usually looks for in a quality trout fishery. To begin with, Big Hunting is visually beautiful. As one drives through the mountains, climbing Route 77 through the Catoctin Mountain National Park, the stream becomes visible on your right. You will see hardwoods and hemlocks all around it and in the adjoining mountains. During the two and a half miles of catch-and-release waters, Big Hunting is lined with rocks, boulders, and little falls. It contains a series of riffles, runs, pocket water, and interesting pools — all holding trout. The rocky bottom always strikes us as jewel-like. This appearance is added to by the abundance of clean gravel, great spawning habitat for trout.

We think of this stream as being divided into two sections. The lower section is called the Canyon, and is located below the Camp Peniel Bridge. As the name implies, this high gradient section of water runs through a steep canyon, with

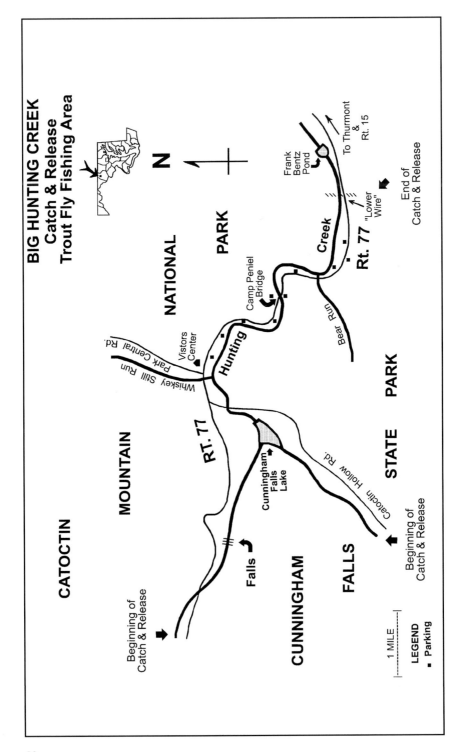

BIG HUNTING CREEK
Catch & Release
Trout Fly Fishing Area

N

CATOCTIN

MOUNTAIN

NATIONAL PARK

Falls

Beginning of Catch & Release

RT. 77

Cunningham Falls Lake

CUNNINGHAM FALLS

STATE PARK

Whiskey Still Run

Park Central Rd.

Vistors Center

Hunting

Camp Peniel Bridge

Bear Run

Creek

Catoctin Hollow Rd.

Beginning of Catch & Release

Rt. 77 "Lower Wire"

Frank Bentz Pond

To Thurmont & Rt. 15

End of Catch & Release

1 MILE

LEGEND
■ Parking

many large boulders, chutes, and runs emptying into deep holes. The upper section, above the bridge, is a bit flatter; but it too contains choice pocket water and plenty of riffles, runs, and holes.

Big Hunting Creek is typically about 20' to 30' wide, and it is well canopied with trees. The hemlocks lining the stream are often quicker to catch your fly than are the sometimes fussy trout that you are seeking. This canopy of course provides shade and helps keep the water cool, a key factor in trout survival during warm Maryland summers.

Although Big Hunting Creek is a stream we have fished and guided on for many years, we met with Rob Gilford in an effort to round out our picture. Rob owns the Rod Rack, a quality fishing store in Frederick, and, like his well-known angler-father, Jim Gilford, he has studied and sought to enhance this fishery for many years.

Rob filled us in on some of the conflict-laden history surrounding the building of Cunningham Falls Lake and its dam on the stream in the late 1960s. The stream on which this lake and dam were built was a great piece of trout water. Due largely to lack of sediment control (as well as the many gallons of diesel fuel emptied into the stream), the building of the dam had a hugely adverse effect on the trout and a devastating impact on insect life for many years. At the present time, though, the fact that the stream is a tailwater may well be a benefit to the insect life and the fishing. The water release policy contains a minimum flow of 1.5 cubic feet per second — surely less than desirable but at least marginally sufficient — and the dam can release water from three different levels. Thus, cold water releases are made in the summer months.

There have been efforts to improve the stream that have also led to controversy. A local group, Friends of Big Hunting Creek, for example, has developed log structures that narrow the stream in a few places and facilitate flow (and thus oxygenation). These efforts have aimed at aiding trout during low flow conditions typical in summer. Others have argued, though, that the structures create an artificial appearance and do not help the fish or the hatching. Although the long term effect of such stream improvement cannot yet be known, we do know that trout on this stream are doing well and are plentiful, especially the streambred brown trout.

We should note that Big Hunting Creek runs for several miles below Frank Bentz Pond and the catch-and-release stretch before it flows into the Monocacy River. This stretch is not stocked, but contains a supply of both wild and stocked fish that move downstream from the catch-and-release stretch as well as the Pond, which is itself heavily stocked. These waters have a two fish limit, but we encourage anglers to release the wild browns that they have the good fortune of catching.

The Fish and the Fishing

The hallmark of Big Hunting Creek is that it has a high density of trout, big trout, different kinds of trout, and some wild trout that are as beautiful as you will see anywhere. The state provides local clubs (Maryland Fly Anglers and Potomac Valley Fly Anglers) with fingerlings. These groups grow and then stock the fish in Big Hunting Creek, about 1000 annually in recent years.

When clients we guide want to try their hand at a big fish, Hunting Creek is usually our choice. Rainbows and brookies are stocked, and the stockies are often very large. In fact, our guess is that the average size for rainbows is about 15". Rainbows in the 18" range are not uncommon, at least until the dead of summer, when these big fellows tend to have trouble. The brookies are of course smaller, but are still very large for brook trout. Although these are stocked fish, they become educated pretty fast, since Big Hunting Creek gets more than its share of fishing pressure. Thus, the term "dumb stockies" does not fit these fish at all, at least not after their first few weeks in the stream. The fish in Big Hunting Creek are challenging and many seem to have earned doctoral degrees in the art of teaching fly anglers humility.

There is a healthy population of streambred brown trout here. They average about 8-10" but often are much larger. This particular strain of brown trout has large red spots, mixed with a blue hue. Speaking personally, we have not seen a prettier brown trout in any other river we have ever fished. To maintain the wild trout population, no brown trout are stocked in Big Hunting Creek. Thus, any brown you catch will be a wild fish. Although these wild fish will take a fly as readily or perhaps even more readily than stocked fish, they are extremely spooky. In fact, if you walk along the stream at a normal pace, you will probably never catch a brown, and the only ones you will get even glimpses of are those scurrying away.

The holdover rate of the wild fish is excellent, even in hot summers that have little rain. They are a hardy population. The rainbows also seem to hold well, and in fact seem to be reproducing, at least marginally. Like the browns, and unlike most rainbows, the bows that have been stocked in Big Hunting Creek tend to be fall spawners. It is quite exciting to slowly walk up Big Hunting Creek in October and November, and see spawning rainbows and browns on their redds.

The stocked brookies do not seem to do so well. Most do not make it through the summer, and those that do so tend to be pretty emaciated by the end of winter. At the same time, many anglers prize the opportunity to catch and release big rainbows, brookies, and wild browns in a single day — a grand slam of sorts.

Fly fishing Big Hunting Creek can be a thrill, and it is also challenging. This is a great stream on which to sight fish. Because it contains a rocky bottom, the water is usually quite clear, and if you look carefully (through a good pair of polarized lenses), the fish are visible. At the same time, you too are visible. Because of this, except in high water conditions (e.g., after heavy spring rains), you will want to take a careful, slow, upstream approach. Dull colored attire in most months is a must, and camo is not a bad idea. It is always a bit funny to see brightly clad anglers fishing downstream *into the fish* on Big Hunting, wondering where all the fish have gone! As noted, the wild browns are especially spooky in these often thin waters. Especially in the low flow of summer and fall, we advise anglers with the old maxim: "Walk as slowly as possible, and then cut that in half!"

Big Hunting Creek's greatest asset is pocket water.

Big Hunting Creek is an excellent place for a wide variety of fly fishing approaches: dry flies, nymphs, streamers, midges, terrestrials. They all work, although what works, where and when on this piece of water can only be learned with experience and patience. Beware, though, of the deep pools with a number of visible fish in them. Unless the fish are actively feeding, don't stay at these holes too long. You won't catch much more than a headache. At such pools (the famed Green Drake Hole, the Elbow Pool, the Bridge pool), streamer fishing is largely a waste of time. Midge fishing, though, can be productive, even when the fish do not seem to be on the feed.

As we noted earlier, sight fishing is not only possible but desirable on this stream. In fact, Big Hunting Creek is a great place to learn to sight nymph. Charlie spent one entire autumn doing this by going to the stream with nymphs *only*. Learning to detect visually the very subtle movements that are telltale signs of a trout taking a nymph can be a great reward on this stream.

Regarding equipment, this is a classic small rod stream. Eight foot rods are about the maximum, given the tight spaces and trees all around you. Long leaders are often a hindrance, as we rarely use anything longer than a 7-1/2' leader (adding tippets of varying lengths, depending on what flies we are fishing). As we have said, drab clothing is a good idea, and polarized lenses are a must. Hip boots are all you will need here, and in the summer months, many anglers like to wet wade this stream.

Hatches, Other Stream Life, and Effective Patterns

There is an abundance of insect life on Big Hunting Creek. While no single dominant hatch occurs, the hatching can be spectacular. At times, it appears that a little of everything seems to be popping off the water. There is such a wide range of hatches that the trout generally seem to be feeding on something. Rob Gilford has studied hatching on the stream for years, and his comments have supplemented our own studies. The year gets off to a wonderful start with the tiny black winter stonefly (#16-20) hatch throughout the colder months. Sunny winter days really get these insects hatching and trout feeding on them. When this occurs, Hunting Creek fish can be quite selective. Adult and nymph patterns both are effective at different times. Watch what the fish are doing. When fish are taking underneath, we like a little black nymph (#18 or 20) that Charlie naturally calls Charlie's Nymph (see Chapter 13).

This hatch is followed by the larger brown stonefly (#14) emergence, running through April. April also ushers in the first of the mayflies, often called the "spring grays." Blue quills (#16-18), and quill Gordons (#14) all appear in April, with sufficient hatching to activate the trout. These are followed by somewhat spotty hatches of March browns (#10-12), gray foxes (#12), and then light cahills (#14-16) in May. Throughout all of these hatches, same-named fly patterns may be used that represent the naturals of both dun and nymph. Add the ever-effective Adams (#14-18) and an assortment of Gold-Ribbed Hare's Ears (#12-18) and beadhead nymphs, and your selection of mayfly patterns will do just fine on Big Hunting Creek.

Big Hunting is also a dynamite caddis stream, and the caddis begin hatching in earnest in April. Darker caddis seem more prominent early in the year, and increasingly lighter naturals appear as the season progresses. Elk Hair Caddis patterns (#14-18) are excellent, especially in pocket water, riffles, and runs. Still pools call for more realistic imitations, e.g., Henryville Specials and other realistic patterns (see Chapter 13). Caddis larva patterns (#14-20), especially in varying

The Elbow Pool, one of Big Hunting Creek's premier pools.

shades of olive, also take many fish. Rob Gilford noted that the Little Yellow Sally (#16-18) seems to be hatching well in recent years during May and June. This is a yellow stonefly that trout like a lot.

During the summer and fall months, terrestrials work great on Big Hunting. Ants (both black and cinnamon, #16-22), Beetles (#16-18), and Crickets (#10-14) are our favorites. And don't forget the "inchworm hatch" in summer and fall. Both floating and sinking inchworms can be tremendously effective patterns.

A fly that seems to work especially well on Big Hunting Creek is the Honey Bug (#14-18), a simple fly consisting of honey bug yarn wrapped over the shank, and a tail made of thread from the yarn or crystal flash. In the colors white or cream, this fly seems to resemble many of the white-ish, grublike critters that inhabit the stream bottom. Larry has had some days on Big Hunting in which it seemed like trout wouldn't stay away from this pattern. Not all days are like that!

Finally, you can do some great midge fishing on Big Hunting Creek. The itsy-bitsies (#20-28) are underfished on this stream, and they can be incredibly effective. Griffith's Gnat patterns on the surface, and various midge pupa and emerger patterns all can entice fussy trout that will not be suckered by your larger patterns. Look for quiet pools where fish are feeding on the surface or underneath, and the chances are good that midge patterns will move those fish. We have found that in such pools, for example, midge larva fished deep will take fish even at times when trout just seem to be sitting on the bottom. (See Chapter 13 for effective midge patterns.)

*Big Hunting Creek delivers gold to angler Mark Gay – a 15"
wild brown trout.*

The Stream and Its Problems

We believe that Big Hunting Creek is just about what one could hope for in
a small mountain freestoner. As we have discussed, it has much beauty, lots of
fish, big fish, and excellent hatching. The stream is easy to wade and easy to walk.

There are paths along most of it, and the banks are easily negotiated even in spots where there are no paths. In fact, one might consider this stream a lazy man's (or woman's) delight.

Big Hunting Creek does have a few problems that are worth noting. Although the minimum water release from the dam of 1.5 cubic feet per second is what we have termed "marginally sufficient," it is clearly less than desirable to sustain the density of wild and stocked fish in this stream. In summer months, it seems that the stream is down to a trickle, although a closer look reveals many cool and aerated holding areas. Be that as it may, we believe that the holdover rate would be significantly improved if the minimum release was even slightly raised. A related problem is that there does not seem to be quite enough natural feed in this stream to sustain both the wild and stocked trout population at as high a rate as many would like. Although insect life is abundant, there does not appear to be as much additional aquatic life as contained in the state's other top streams, e.g., crayfish, daces, sculpins. There is no easy solution to this problem. One can stock fewer especially large fish, continue to work on stream improvements that will result in even more insect life, or simply live with the problem, which probably most anglers believe isn't too hard to live with given the good supply of fish and the quality fishing.

Another small problem for some anglers is that the stream is within earshot of Route 77 throughout much of the catch-and-release stretch. Thus, one can hear cars driving past. Personally, we find it so easy to get lost in our fishing that we rarely hear the traffic. But the road does reduce the sense of being away from it all.

Location and Access Points

The Special Area is located above the town of Thurmont, which is off Route 15 between the towns of Frederick and Gettysburg, PA. When you get to Thurmont, take Route 77 off 15. Go west (right) at the stop sign after the exit and the catch-and-release section will appear on your right in a couple of miles, immediately after you pass Frank Bentz Pond. Parking areas are plentiful along the entire catch-and-release stretch, and each is just a short distance from the water.

As you travel along the stream, the first bridge you will cross is the Camp Peniel Bridge, which, as we have said, divides the upper and lower parts of the stream. There are parking lots on both sides of the bridge, and this is a good place to park if you want to access both the upper and lower parts of Big Hunting Creek. As you drive up Route 77 in about a mile you will see the Catoctin Mountain National Park Visitor Center, which contains information about the Park and adjoining areas. Almost across the street from the Visitor Center is the Joe Brooks Memorial. On the Memorial is the Creed of the Brotherhood of the Jungle Cock, dated 1940. The Creed is worth repeating:

— We who love angling, in order that it may enjoy, practice, and reward to the later generations, mutually move together toward a common goal — the conservation and restoration of American game fishes.

— Toward this end we pledge that our creel limits shall always be less than the legal restrictions and always well within the bounty of nature herself.

— Enjoying, as we do, only a life estate in the out of doors, and morally charged in our time with the responsibility of handing it down unspoiled to tomorrow's inheritors, we individually undertake annually to take at least one boy a-fishing, instructing him, as best we know, in the responsibilities that are soon to be wholly his.

— Holding that moral law transcends the legal statutes, always beyond the deeds of any one man, and holding that example alone is the one certain teacher, we pledge always to conduct ourselves in such fashion on the stream as to make safe for others the heritage which is ours and theirs.

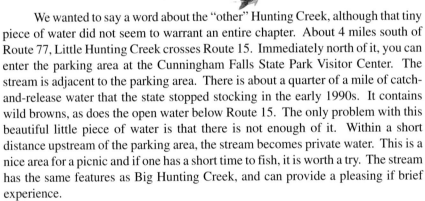

Addendum: Little Hunting Creek

We wanted to say a word about the "other" Hunting Creek, although that tiny piece of water did not seem to warrant an entire chapter. About 4 miles south of Route 77, Little Hunting Creek crosses Route 15. Immediately north of it, you can enter the parking area at the Cunningham Falls State Park Visitor Center. The stream is adjacent to the parking area. There is about a quarter of a mile of catch-and-release water that the state stopped stocking in the early 1990s. It contains wild browns, as does the open water below Route 15. The only problem with this beautiful little piece of water is that there is not enough of it. Within a short distance upstream of the parking area, the stream becomes private water. This is a nice area for a picnic and if one has a short time to fish, it is worth a try. The stream has the same features as Big Hunting Creek, and can provide a pleasing if brief experience.

CHAPTER 7
OWENS CREEK
Delayed Harvest in Reverse

F or those who enjoy catch-and-release fishing, this Catoctin Mountain freestoner is one of Maryland's best success stories. For many years, Owens Creek was a put-and-take fishery. Yet, as we knew back in the 1970s when we began fishing in Maryland, this little gem has a good holdover rate and some natural reproduction. This made it a natural for special regulations. However, there was a big problem. Once a stream in a state with relatively few streams has been designated as put-and-take, the conversion to catch-and-release causes a lot of agitation among anglers who enjoy keeping fish. Naturally, they feel that something valuable has been taken away from them. As a response, the Maryland DNR has wisely sought to offer new put-and-take opportunities to anglers whenever they turn an area into a catch-and-release water.

Given Owens Creek's potential, and the lack of any new fishing opportunities in exchange for taking this stream away from anglers who were accustomed to harvesting fish, a creative solution was called for. And the state's enlightened DNR people came up with one. A "reverse delayed harvest" regulation was created on the most fishable section of the stream. Thus, a sizeable portion of the stream allows anglers their five-per-day limit from March 1 through May 31. Then on June 1 — the point at which most anglers who fish for food have disappeared from Maryland streams anyhow — the special regulations kick in. At that point, the regulation changes to catch-and-release until the following March, with only flies and lures permitted. In the spring, heavy stocking occurs, with the fish being mostly rainbows. Then in June, when catch-and-release begins, more trout are stocked. This June stocking consists of mostly brown trout because of the brown's superior holdover capacity. Trout (usually browns) are also sometimes stocked again in the fall, depending on water level.

The special regulation section covers about five miles, from Raven Rock Road downstream to Roddy Road. Owens eventually flows into the Monocacy River. Stocking is done from the white church next to the road at Lantz down to the covered bridge.

The stream originates from mountain springs and flows through the Catoctin Mountain National Park, continues through farmlands, meadows, and through woodlands with a steep gradient. The scenery is lovely throughout its course. Owens contains classic riffles and runs, nice pocket water, and some very productive pools. The bottom is mostly gravel, cobbles, and large boulders. This little freestoner averages about 25' in width, but varies from 15-60'.

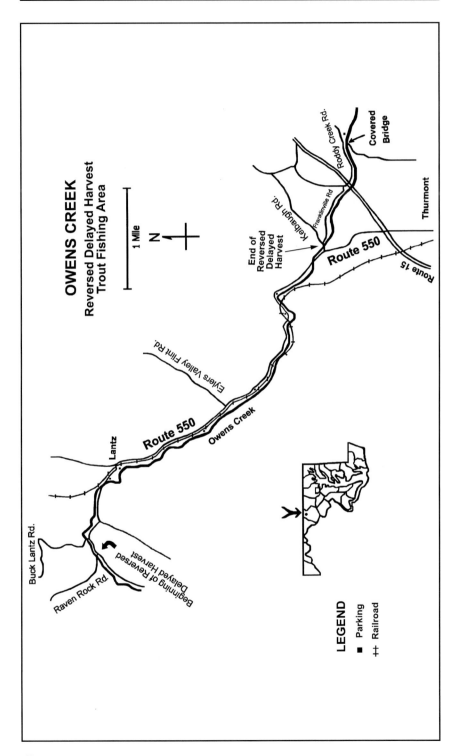

OWENS CREEK
Reversed Delayed Harvest
Trout Fishing Area

1 Mile

N

Roddy Creek Rd.

Covered Bridge

Franklinville Rd.

Kelbaugh Rd.

Thurmont

End of Reversed Delayed Harvest

Route 550

Route 15

Eylers Valley Flint Rd.

Lantz

Route 550

Owens Creek

Buck Lantz Rd.

Raven Rock Rd.

Beginning of Reversed Delayed Harvest

LEGEND
■ Parking
++ Railroad

The Fish and the Fishing

As noted, the special area of Owens is stocked with browns and rainbows, mostly in the 10-14" range. However, we have seen browns in the 18" range there, even in the fall, and DNR electroshocking recently discovered a 22" submarine.

Reproduction of browns does occur throughout the special section. We should add that the waters upstream of the special section, up to the stream's headwaters, contain reproducing browns and brook trout. These upper waters, with a two fish per day limit, are very skinny, and require a careful approach. Most anglers who fish them release their catches, which is a good idea. This is a fragile resource, and it could be easily decimated if anglers regularly kept their catch.

We like smaller rods on Owens, usually 6-1/2 to 8' rods, with line weights from 2-5. Leaders of 7-1/2' are effective, and tippet size will vary with water conditions. When the water gets low, e.g., in summer and fall, 6 and 7X may be required for success on the surface. That is because the low waters of summer and fall, especially when gin clear, make trout very leader shy.

Hip boots are all you really need on this mountain stream. A good pair of polarized lenses is invaluable, since at least some of the fishing you do can be sight fishing. Because this is small water, a careful upstream approach is indicated. Even though Owens Creek is small and is fairly canopied by trees, there is a sense of openness. Thus, fly casting can be a pleasure. At the same time, it is not as open as other rivers (e.g., the Gunpowder), so you do need to take care.

How good is the holdover rate? Charlie fished this water during one of the worst autumn droughts the state had ever experienced. The water was frightfully low, and trout had not been stocked since June. Fish (including wild fish) were everywhere, and rose freely in deeper pools. Small flies (Griffith's Gnats and Three-Hackles, #18-22; see Chapter 13) and light tippets (6X and 7X) took many fish. To boot, the trout were fat and sassy.

Hatches, Other Stream Life, and Effective Patterns

The hatching situation is fairly typical for an eastern mountain stream. Although no spectacular hatches occur, there are enough things happening to keep the fish looking up. A nice tiny black winter stonefly (#16-20) followed by a larger brown stonefly (#14-16) gets the year off to a good start in the first three months. Green and yellow stoneflies (#14-16) hatch well into June.

Small hatches of the "April grays" (quill gordons, blue quills, and dark hendricksons) continue into June (especially the blue quill). You can see some March Browns (#10) in May, light cahills (#14) in June, and blue-winged olives (#16-20) from about June through the fall. A variety of caddisflies appear on Owens, with tannish colors occurring in June (#14) and proceeding to greenish rhyocophila (#14) and then darker colors (with mottled wings) toward fall.

A picturesque view of Owens Creek.

Grayish-black midges can be seen throughout the year. Ants and beetles (#14-20) provide great summer fishing.

Although Owens has the usual range of forage fish (e.g., dace, sculpins, darters), there is one surprise. Susan Rivers, a biologist who studies insect life on waters throughout Maryland, notes the good population of scuds (fresh water "shrimp"). These are orange colored with a pink accent, and range in size from #14-18. Scud imitations work well on Owens.

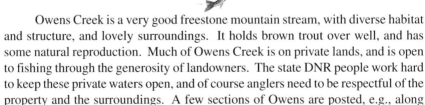

The River and Its Problems

Owens Creek is a very good freestone mountain stream, with diverse habitat and structure, and lovely surroundings. It holds brown trout over well, and has some natural reproduction. Much of Owens Creek is on private lands, and is open to fishing through the generosity of landowners. The state DNR people work hard to keep these private waters open, and of course anglers need to be respectful of the property and the surroundings. A few sections of Owens are posted, e.g., along Foxville-Deerfield Road. Look for posted signs and the DNR fishing signs.

Owens Creek's most notable problem is that the water does get pretty warm in the dead of summer. John Mullican, DNR biologist notes, for example, that temperatures may peak in the upper 70s during a heat wave on a July afternoon. On a "normal" summer, peak temps will be in the mid 70s, and of course cooling occurs in the evenings. Because of this, it is best to fish in the early mornings and again in the evenings on this stream, as well as most Maryland freestoners.

Location and Access Points

Much of the special regulation section runs along Route 550. To get to the stream, take Md. Route 15 to Route 550, which is about 1 mile north of Thurmont (Frederick County). Go west on Route 550, and within a short distance you will cross the stream. Look for the DNR regulation signs on trees. There are a number of pullovers as you drive along the stream. As you move upstream, Owens bends away from the road. The gradient of the stream increases as you walk further away from the road into the more remote section.

As you drive toward the village of Lantz, the stream parallels railroad tracks. Interestingly, with the help of volunteers, the DNR uses a rail mounted truck on these tracks to distribute fish. This results in the fish being nicely spread out on this section of the creek. This is a good section to fish as summer heats up. It is well canopied with trees, and the water is usually a few degrees cooler than the flatter sections downstream.

It has been exciting to see how the implementation of "reverse delayed harvest" has affected the fishing on Owens Creek. Hopefully this enlightened approach can serve as a model for changes on other streams that have good hold-over rates and some reproduction.

Part II

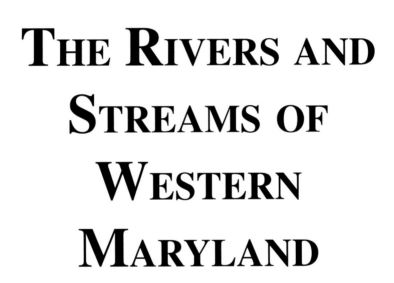

The Rivers and Streams of Western Maryland

CHAPTER 8
TOWN CREEK

A Secluded Stream with Little Pressure

Although Town Creek has been a special regulation stream for five years as of this writing, little is known about it. That is because it is one of the state's most remote streams, and some of its best holding water is not as easily accessed as in most other streams. Located within the Green Ridge State Forest, this is a low gradient creek, with lots of interesting structure and a good flow until summer. The width of this stream is usually about 30-50'. There are two different special regulation (delayed harvest) stretches on the creek, each covering about 1-2 miles of water (see map).

Regarding structure, there are some long pools (e.g., 50-100 yards), many deep pockets off slate ridges, and flat riffles. You will also encounter dead falls and roots systems that tend to hold fish. The flow of this creek varies a great deal according to the season. In the spring, the flow is heavy, and some of the best spots are difficult to wade. By summer, the water is generally too low (and warm) for trout to survive. The summer temperatures can get as high as the low 80s.

Because of low flows and warming water as summer approaches, Town Creek has been designated as a delayed harvest stream. Catch-and-release is in effect until June 15. Only artificial lures and flies are permitted. On June 16, the regulation shifts to a creel limit of two fish per day, and there are no special bait or lure restrictions. This policy holds until October 1, when it shifts back to catch-and-release, lures and flies only.

If you fish Town Creek in the spring, you'll see an abundance of wildflowers. Acres of bluebells will be apparent, as well as wild bleeding hearts. You will also encounter lots of wildlife — grouse, turkey, and deer are plentiful around this stream. In fact, it is likely that you will see more wildlife than anglers. Because of the remoteness of Town Creek, plus the fact that there are no easy paths or roads along the stream as it traverses through farmland and forest, this is one of the few Maryland streams that has been *underfished*.

The Fish and The Fishing

Town Creek is stocked by the state with rainbow and brown trout. Rainbows are usually stocked in the spring, and browns in the fall if there is sufficient water flow. There is a high density of stocked fish in the delayed harvest section, most

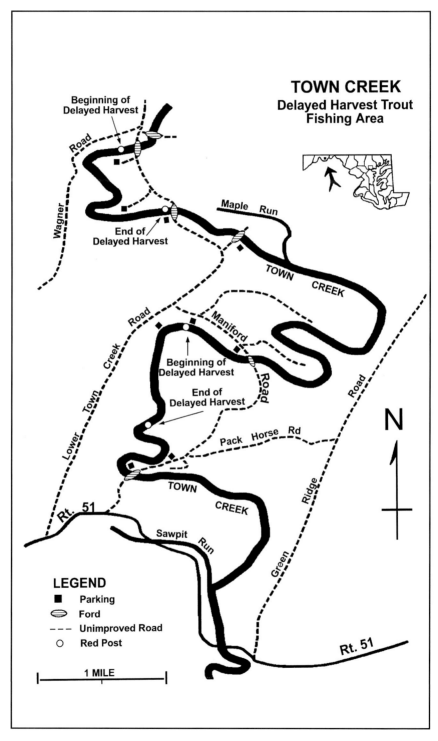

TOWN CREEK
Delayed Harvest Trout
Fishing Area

Beginning of
Delayed Harvest

Road

Maple Run

Wagner

End of
Delayed Harvest

TOWN CREEK

Road

Maniford

Beginning of
Delayed Harvest

Creek

Town

Road

End of
Delayed Harvest

Lower

Pack Horse Rd

Road

N

Ridge

Rt. 51

TOWN CREEK

Green

Sawpit Run

Rt. 51

LEGEND
■ Parking
⊖ Ford
--- Unimproved Road
○ Red Post

1 MILE

being in the 10-12" range, but with some large fish up to about 18". Due to low summer flows and high temps, there is no reproduction, and little summer hold-over. However, the browns that are stocked after the catch-and-release policy again kicks in on October 1 will often hold over into the next summer.

Regarding gear, chest waders are best when the spring runs are highest, although hip boots are fine for the rest of the year. In the winter and early spring, a longer rod is a good idea because you will likely be doing a lot of streamer fishing. A 9' for 5 wt. is ideal during this season. After early spring, though, an 8' for 4 wt. is an excellent choice. At the same time, we need to underscore that this is the kind of stream that allows for rod lengths and line weights of virtually any size at any time. Whatever rod you use, the casting situation is very comfortable. There is enough openness to permit easy casting, despite the fact that we would classify Town Creek as a relatively small stream.

As we have said, during winter and again following the spring stocking, Town Creek is best fished with an assortment of streamer patterns (see next section). Once the spring hatches kick in, and the trout become acclimated to insect life (and begin to feed on insects), you can effectively use dry flies and nymphs. When nymphing, Town Creek is an especially good stream on which to use strike indicators. In fact, the moderate flows and deeper pools make nymphing without a strike indicator difficult. You can use a big (#8-10) dry fly as an indicator (the trout at times will whack this surface pattern), or any of the strike indicators that are commonly available.

Hatches, Other Stream Life, and Effective Patterns

Although there appears to be good hatching on Town Creek, little detailed information is available about specific hatches. Dick Sluss, who fishes the stream often, notes that there are moderately good caddis hatches beginning around April. Tan and olive caddis (#14-18) appear then and continue sporadically through summer. The other hatches Don notes are Dobsonflies (#6-8; hellgrammites), craneflies (#14-16), and midges (#20-24, gray and cream). The craneflies, in particular, are abundant and are usually an underrated source of trout food. If you tie your own flies, a good cranefly pattern includes (a) a pale yellow body, (b) gray rooster wing tips tied delta style (laid flat on back and splayed to a 45 degree angle) or alternatively, gray zelon tied flat on back caddis style; and (c) 3-4 turns of over-sized hackle (2-3 times the hook gap) in the thorax, to imitate the very long legs of the cranefly.

Regarding effective patterns, in the spring Woolly Buggers (#10-12, especially black or olive) are the ticket, perhaps because they roughly approximate the abundant hellgrammites that are present. Various caddis patterns are also effective once the caddises start hatching in spring. Try fishing the pupa as well as the adult pattern. Olive/green pupa patterns are especially good. Bead head caddis patterns are deadly at this time, and don't go to the stream without some soft hackles (with olive, pale yellow, or tan bodies), both with and without bead heads. These soft hackles can effectively imitate caddises as well as craneflies.

Especially in the early spring but also at other times, patterns such as the San Juan Worm (#14-16), Honeybug (#14-16), and Glo Bugs (#8-10) can be incredibly effective. We have found that Glo Bugs or egg patterns are especially appealing to trout when white glo bug yarn is tied in at the thorax, and allowed to drape over the "egg" that forms the body of the fly.

Although there are some mayfly hatches on Town Creek, not enough has been observed to allow for very detailed information. Clearly, more observation on hatches is needed.

The River and Its Problems

Town Creek is a low gradient stream that provides excellent fishing into early summer. It meanders through remote woodland located within state forest land. Because of this, as well as difficult access, Town Creek offers the angler some solitude, and an opportunity to get away from it all.

The problems with Town Creek are in part typical for delayed harvest stretches: low and warming summer flows, no reproduction, and limited holdover through summer. The lack of a good canopy of trees on many portions of the creek is a problem. Not having the cover that such a canopy creates is no doubt a major cause of water warming. Pollution caused by farming practices is also a big problem. The Allegany County Soil Conservation Service has worked hard with land owners to rectify the problems. Projects aimed at bank buffering and live-stock control (e.g., fencing, cattle crossings) have been effectively conducted. These great efforts need to be continued.

Location and Access Points: How to Get There

Before giving directions to the stream, we want to caution anglers about the so-called low water fords in the upper delayed harvest section. The lower ford of that section, in particular, seems to us to be unsafe to drive across, even in low flow situations. When fishing this upper section, look for parking pullovers rather than crossing the fords with your vehicle, as some published directions may suggest.

The most straightforward way to get to Town Creek is to take Route 51 south from I-68 at Cumberland. Stay on Route 51 for 18-19 miles. At this point, you hit Lower Town Creek Road. Make a left and continue on Lower Town Creek Road and go 2.5 miles until you reach Maniford Road. Make a right onto Maniford Road, and in less than a mile you will reach the State Forest parking area. The lower delayed harvest section is located between this parking area and an incon-spicuous red post about 1.75 miles downstream.

To access the upper delayed harvest section, continue on Lower Town Creek Road past Maniford Road for about a mile. Here you approach the low water ford we have noted. Look for pullovers rather than driving across the ford. The delayed harvest section is from this point upstream for about two miles. You can hike to the upper part of this upper section, walking along Lower Town Creek Road for about a half a mile to an unmarked gate entrance on the left. Town Creek is a few yards from that point. The upper delayed harvest section, like the lower one, has red posts demarcating its boundaries.

You can also access this upper delayed harvest section from I-68. Take exit 56 south (Williams Road) at the town of Flintstone. In approximately 200 yards, you run into Route 144. Go left (east) on Route 144 for 1-2 miles to Warm Springs Road. Take a right onto Warm Springs, and stay on it for 1-2 miles. Then make a left onto Town Creek Road, and stay on this road for about 5 miles. Make a left onto Lower Town Creek Road. The stream will be on your left. Look for pullovers along the stream. You will also encounter fords. Once again, be wary about driving across these, especially in the spring.

CHAPTER 9
THE SAVAGE RIVER
Maryland's Hatch Factory

T he special regulation section of the Savage River runs for what may be the most fertile four-mile stretch of water in Maryland. Located in Garrett County, within the 53,000-acre Savage River State Forest, these special regulation waters begin at the Savage Reservoir dam, and run for about four miles before emptying into the North Branch of the Potomac River. The Savage also has a section above the Reservoir that is managed as a put-and-take fishery, with a creel limit of five fish per day. In this chapter we focus on the four-mile special reg section, although a few comments are also offered about the fishery above the Reservoir.

The special regulation section is managed as a Trophy Trout area, where the angler can keep two trout per day — brook trout 12 inches or over and brown trout 18 inches or over. Anglers who fish the Savage, however, usually release everything they catch, a policy we heartily endorse. Within this trophy section, there are two sets of tackle requirements. From the dam to the lower suspension bridge, called the Allegheny Bridge, only fly fishing is permitted. This fly fishing section covers about 1.25 miles. Below the Allegheny Bridge, both lures and flies are permitted. This part of the river covers about 2.75 miles before joining the North Branch.

The trophy section is one of the highest gradient waters in the state, and the gradient creates some interesting structure — lots of fast water, including riffles, runs, rapids, and chutes. The river is usually about 50-70' wide, and has water of varying depth, partly depending on the water release at the dam. Regardless of the release, though, you can find deep pools along with the faster water. Even in low release situations, for example, some of the deeper pools are over the head of your average tall person. As you fish the Savage, look around and you'll see banks lined with hemlock trees and rhododendron, some rock walls, and large boulders on the bank as well as in the river. The beauty of the surroundings is enhanced by fishing in a miniature gorge, lined with ledges and bluffs.

Because it is a tailwater, and because the Maryland DNR successfully negotiated a bottom-release from the dam, the water temperatures are generally ideal for trout and for fishing. They rarely get above the mid-60s in the dead of summer, and are generally above 40 degrees in the coldest sections (near the mouth) in the dead of winter. These temperatures make for year-round fishing, provided that the angler can withstand the cold western Maryland air temperatures in the winter. Along with nearly ideal water temperatures, the water quality of the river is excellent. One good indication of quality is pH level. Influenced by the geological

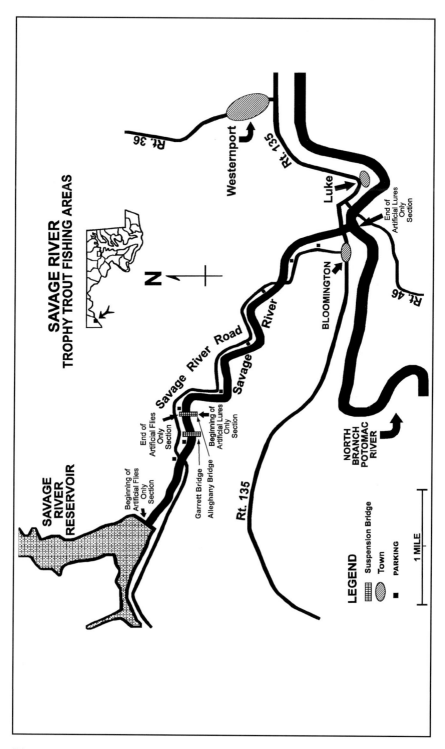

SAVAGE RIVER
TROPHY TROUT FISHING AREAS

N

SAVAGE RIVER RESERVOIR

Savage River Road

Savage River

Beginning of Artificial Flies Only Section

End of Artificial Flies Only Section

Garrett Bridge
Alleghany Bridge

Beginning of Artificial Lures Only Section

Rt. 135

Westernport

Rt. 36

Rt. 135

Luke

End of Artificial Lures Only Section

Rt. 46

BLOOMINGTON

NORTH BRANCH POTOMAC RIVER

LEGEND
Suspension Bridge
Town
PARKING

1 MILE

formations in the mountains above the Savage Reservoir, the pH level of the Savage is slightly above 7, which is comparable to the best freestone streams. Given the temperatures and water quality, trout naturally do well in this river, as do the aquatic life that trout like to eat!

If there is a single word that we believe captures the Savage River, it is *diversity*. This diversity is seen in the river's structure and holding water, its insect life, its trout, its difficulty level, and, just as important for the angler, its water flow. We shall explore each of these types of diversity at various points in the chapter. Regarding structure and holding water, there is every water situation imaginable on the Savage. We have noted that the high gradient produces many rapids, chutes, riffles, and runs. There are also long glides, deep pools, and eddies (including what we call "micro-eddies", which seem to be just about everywhere). Because there is premiere holding water in all of the structural conditions we have mentioned, trout seem to hold everywhere and anywhere on the river. This creates one of the happiest "problems" that an angler will ever face. Where do you cast in such a situation? You can take your pick! (Naturally, the answer partly depends on the fly patterns you are using, e.g., surface flies, nymphs, or streamers — see section on hatches and patterns.)

The Savage is an easily accessed river. Savage River Road parallels it through-out its course, and there are many parking spots along the road (see map). Unlike many rivers with roads running alongside them, one's solitude is not diminished by the sound of traffic. The sound of running water, sometimes rushing and some-times gliding, drowns out the noise of traffic, except perhaps for the sounds of occasional logging trucks.

Another form of diversity pertains to the river's varying flows, a phenomenon that is directly tied to the amount of water released at the dam. In the old days, major water releases occurred due to Olympic whitewater events and training for those events. These had a significant and adverse effect of the fish and the insect life. Olympic events and training no longer occur on the Savage, but there are still times when the river is essentially unfishable due to recreational whitewater releases. Because of this, we urge you to find out the water level before heading for the river. The number to call is 410-962-7687. When flows get higher than 150 cubic feet per second (cfs), the river becomes extremely hard to fish. Many anglers like the cfs to be between 50 and 100 cfs, and efforts are made to keep the flow at 50 cfs or greater. During drought conditions, the cfs can get below that figure. For example, we have fished the river at 30 cfs, and the fishing was dynamite. Because we were accustomed to fishing freestone streams that get *really* low in the summer, 30 cfs seemed like a lot of water to us.

The Fish and the Fishing

The great diversity we have noted also pertains to the kinds of trout in the Savage, as well as fishing tactics on this river. Regarding the trout, the first thing to make note of is that no stocking occurs in this section of the river. The river contains reproducing populations of brown trout and brookies. Eight or ten years ago, the brookies far outnumbered the browns, but the situation has reversed in recent years. As the river tumbles toward its mouth, it also contains some rainbows and cutthroat trout that had been stocked in the North Branch of the Potomac. Thus, you have the chance at an unusual eastern grand slam — browns, brookies, rainbows, and cutthroats in the same day.

There are some nice sized brook trout in the Savage. While these little fighters average about 7-10 inches, it is not uncommon to catch brookies in the 12-inch range. The brownies are naturally bigger than the brook trout, averaging about 10-12 inches. Browns in the 14-inch range are not unusual, though, and now and then you can hook into a brown in the 18-20 range. Although the average fish in the Savage is not large, it is both strong and beautiful. Because of the swift current, the abundant food supply, and the healthy water, fish in the Savage are very strong and feisty. A 12" brownie will give the fly rodder quite a tussle, and feel like a much bigger fish. Both brooks and browns are radiantly colored, with each looking like a multicolored jewel.

The rainbows and cutthroats that run up the Savage from the North Branch can get quite large. As we discuss in the North Branch chapter, many were stocked as fingerlings, so that they have all the characteristics of a wild fish.

There is a high density of trout in the Savage, with recent studies revealing about 84 lbs. per acre. This density is about as high as any wild trout population in any river in Maryland, and it is in the same range as any river we have fished, anywhere! We recall fishing the river on one very warm summer afternoon — a time when we would not expect to see trout, no less see trout taking surface flies. At one small pool with a good run emptying into it, we spotted well over 15 fish, some of them sizable. Among these trout, at least ten of them were taking insects off the surface.

The difficulty level of the fishing on the Savage is quite variable, although on the whole this is a demanding river to fly fish. Our impression is that the average angler will come away from a morning's fishing with a few trout. The fish have become educated in recent years, and the abundance of natural food in the river makes them quite fussy about what they will inhale. There are certain pools and glides that are as exacting as any difficult limestoner we have ever fished. Jay Sheppard, who fishes the Savage often and ardently, comments that in some pools the fish are able to identify the manufacturer of your hooks, to say nothing of the names of your flies! For example, the trout who reside in the pools immediately above and below the upper suspension bridge (Garrett Bridge), are pretty much constantly sipping insects on the surface, but catching these critters requires highly technical fishing, e.g., 15' leaders tapered to 7 or 8X tippet, sparsely tied and realistic fly patterns, and extremely careful wading (to prevent the water from rippling, which will put the fish down). Jay refers to one of the Savage's difficult pools, the one right above the upper Savage River Road bridge, as the Ph.D. pool. Sometimes we think that trout at this educational level were put on the earth to give fly anglers humility.

Over time the Savage River has carved its way through the forest to contribute its collection of H_2O to the Potomac River.

Having said that, there are times and situations during which the fishing can be a lot easier than we have indicated. On some days, you can take a size 14 elk hair caddis pattern, fish the pocket water, and have a 25 fish day. Generally, the fish are going to be much more catchable in the pocket water than the pools and glides. You can do tight line nymphing in the pockets, using your favorite nymph, and often do quite well. In essence, there are fishing situations on the Savage to fit just about everyone — from the very seasoned fly rodder who wants a challenge and prefers highly technical fishing to the angler who is just beginning his or her fly fishing career.

We think there is a common misperception of the Savage that it is a better nymphing river than dry fly river. To the contrary, after the big water releases from the dam occur in spring, this river can be dry fly heaven. Due to the great hatches, there always seem to be trout rising somewhere from April into winter. The dry fly enthusiast's job is to find the rising fish. It is not a hard job.

One point worth noting is that if you are fishing in the evening, and are at a good looking hole, it is often best to just hang out there for a while rather than moving on if there are no fish rising. Hatching can trigger surface activity at any time on these good holes, and "waiting it out" can be a whole lot more effective than running from one hole to another.

While dry fly fishing is often great on the Savage, this is also a wonderful nymphing river, with a variety of nymphing methods being effective. We like tight-line nymphing in much of the pocket water, although the use of a strike indicator may be called for when nymphing in the deeper pools and glides. One feature of the river that is a factor when nymphing is the algae that exists on the rocks during most times of the year. This can make for some frustration if you are bouncing your fly on the bottom because the fly often will have algae on it when you bring it out of the water. There are three ways of dealing with this problem: lighten you split shot so the fly does not go to the bottom; use a strike indicator to keep the fly at the optimum level; or just live with the problem. We often do the latter because bouncing nymphs on the bottom is often so effective.

Many fly rodders love to streamer fish in the Savage. Streamers are especially effective because of the abundance of baitfish. The usual techniques are effective on this river, although we have found that the best streamer fishing occurs when the water is high or off colored, and when the temps are colder, e.g., during the winter months.

Regarding tackle, again diversity is the name of the game. For example, fly rods from 6 to 9' are all viable, as are line weights in the 2-5 range. The best rod length and line weight will depend on the kind of fishing you want to do. For example, if you are doing tight line nymphing, an 8 1/2' to 9 ' rod is preferable to shorter ones, and if you are chucking big streamers, a heavier weight line is desirable. If dry fly fishing, on the other hand, lighter lines are the ticket, and rod length is not much of an issue. You can use either a weight forward or double taper fly line. When nymphing, you can readily get the fly down to where the fish live by affixing split shot onto the leader (with the amount of weight and placement of the split shot determined by the depth and velocity of the water).

Leader length and size will also depend on the kind of fishing you are doing, but generally we recommend longer leaders and finer tippets than for most streams. When surface fishing, we rarely use a tippet that is thicker than 5X. Actually, 6X or even 7X is usually preferable. Also, if you are on the surface, 9' leaders in addition to tippets of 2-3' are helpful when dealing with the very complex currents of this river. For subsurface fishing, tippets of 1-2' are sufficient, and 5X is usually a good bet, unless you are using very small nymphs, e.g., #18 and smaller. In the latter instance, you will probably want 6X tippets.

Although you can get away with hip boots, chest waders are preferable. They will allow you to get to significantly more trout lies than will hippers. Whether you use hippers or chest waders, though, one aspect of wading the Savage needs to be boldfaced and underscored. That is, this river is treacherous to wade. This is so because the algae-covered rocks are extremely slippery — we liken them to greased bowling balls — and they never seem to be where they are supposed to be. Also, it seems like every rock in the river is misshapen! At times, each step is an adventure. Because of the difficulties in wading, we strongly recommend that the angler have cleats as well as felt soles. In addition, we think a wading staff is highly desirable, perhaps necessary for most anglers.

The water gauge on the Savage River marks a pool that has Harvard-educated fish. Jay Sheppard has aptly named this the PhD pool.

Hatches, Other Stream Life, and Effective Patterns

The subtitle of this chapter, "Maryland's Hatch Factory," has an obvious basis. The hatch situation on the Savage is probably the best in the state, in terms of both diversity and number of insects. As an example of this diversity, a fishing buddy of ours who is also an expert bug man (and a biologist by training), counted no less than 11 species of mayflies during a single June evening. He also observed four different stoneflies during this same evening, and did not examine either caddises or midges. Another example: During a warm July evening, when fishing a single small pool for a couple of hours, we observed blue-winged olives (#18-20), sulphurs (#16-18), light and dark cahills (#14), Potomanthus (#10), yellow Sally stoneflies (#14), at least three different caddisfly species, and a plethora of midges. In terms of hatching, the Savage is truly a blue ribbon river.

The hatches that occur are pretty typical of your blue ribbon eastern freestoners, except that they are more profuse than most. The tiny black winter stonefly (#16-20) occurring in January through March ushers the year in. (This hatch actually begins in late November). The larger brown stonefly (#14-16) arrives shortly after the black stone, and overlaps with it. On sunny and warm(er) winter days, fishing these hatches can be a blast. (See Chapter 13 for some adult and nymphal patterns can are effective during these hatches.)

During spring, the "April grays" make their appearance in good numbers. The blue quill (#16-20; also called the mahogany dun) and quill Gordon (#12-14) seem to appear first, followed shortly afterward by the fabled Hendrickson (#10-12) and red quill (#14; the male Hendrickson). Nymphs and duns of the same name are effective during these hatches, although an appropriately sized Adams often works just fine. During the Hendrickson hatch, try using some emergers. They can yield surprisingly positive results.

To our mind, once the biggest water releases of spring are diminished, the best hatches kick in. May and June can be fly fishing Nirvana on the Savage, as the water and sky seem to be filled with a dizzying array of insects. March browns (#10), gray foxes (#14), and the coveted green drake (#8-10) all appear in May, and are fishable hatches. Use your favorite same-named nymph and dun patterns during these hatches.

The big sulphur hatch begins in earnest in late May and continues through July. Both the larger (#14-16) and smaller (#18-20) sulphurs make strong appearances, representing three different species of Ephemerella. A size #16 dun pattern works well for all of these, although as the hatch proceeds, the fish get fussier, and more precise imitation are often the ticket. Don't forget the evening spinner falls. They can be spectacular, although as in all good spinner falls, there are often so many naturals on the water that it is hard to catch fish with your imitation.

Patterns at all levels are useful during the sulphur hatch: nymphs, emergers, duns, and spinners. Regarding nymphs, since the sulphur nymph is varying shades of brown, we find the standard Gold-Ribbed Hare's Ear and the Pheasant Tail nymphs to be highly effective. The addition of bead heads to these tried and true patterns at times enhances their effectiveness. However, we have noticed that as fish see more and more bead head patterns, they become wary of them and are often more prone to hit a conventional nymph pattern. As we have noted in earlier chapters, wet flies are generally underrated and specifically so during sulphur hatches. The Little Marryatt (#16), a sulphur wet fly, is often a great fish taker during sulphur season when fish are not taking flies on the surface (see Chapter 13 for recipe.)

Light cahills (and some dark cahills; #12-14) appear a few weeks later than the sulphurs, peak in mid-June, and hatch throughout July. These, in conjunction with the sulphurs, keep the fishing in high gear.

A very important, but underrated, hatch on the Savage is the blue-winged olive emergence. These olives appear throughout much of the year, although the size and time of emergence is dependent on the season. Sizes range from 16 to about 20, with the smaller ones appearing moreso later in the year. Also, while these insects emerge more strongly on cloudy days, they hatch much earlier in the day during the warm summer months. For example, the strongest hatching usually occurs before 7:30 AM in the summer, although you will see a few of these insects (and trout feeding on them) throughout the day, if cloudy.

In June and July, a couple of stoneflies make their appearance in numbers large enough to motivate the fish to feed. The lime Sally but especially the yellow

A 15" brown, framed on the Savage River.

Sally (both about #14) hatch during these times. Yellow and lime elk hair caddis patterns work well for the adults, and we find that yellow soft hackles are especially good subsurface patterns for the nymphal stage.

Caddises are a major source of fish food on the Savage, and are excellent patterns to fish with. These insects appear from about April through early winter. The tan caddis (#14) is the first to hatch, making its appearance in April. This is followed in May by an olive-bodied caddis with tan or gray-brown wings (#14-16) and a gray caddis (#14-16). Some cinnamon caddises (#16, with mottled wings) also emerge in late summer and into the fall. All of these may be imitated with the elk or deer hair caddis patterns. Try hackling only in the thorax rather than palmering through the body, as is customary for the elk hair caddis. This gives a somewhat more realistic look to the fly. When fishing quiet pools with highly selective and fussy trout, try the realistic caddis patterns we present in Chapter 13. We have found these to be the best caddis imitations for the most difficult trout. A range of caddis pupa and larva, including those with beadheads, are effective during caddis emergences.

The usual array of terrestrials (hoppers, crickets, ants, beetles) are effective on the Savage. Beetles and ants are dynamite fish takers beginning in early summer; and hoppers and crickets work best beginning in the dead of summer. One terrestrial worth underscoring is the inchworm. It appears in summer and trout love to feast on it. Try Green Weenies (#14) or San Juan Inchworms (#14). Fish the pocket water with these patterns and you should catch fish. Once they key in on inchworms, trout will take imitations well after the inchworm has stopped dropping on the water, i.e., into early winter.

Because of nutrients stored in and then released from the dam, the Savage has a healthy scud population (also called freshwater shrimp). These crustaceans (#16-18) are especially prominent in the upper section of the special regulation area and are usually a light greenish gray in color. The closer you get to the dam, the more scuds you will find. And the more effective will be your scud imitation.

There are good supplies of daces, sculpins, and crayfish in this river. Fly patterns of the same names are effective throughout the year, and are especially potent in winter, early spring, and again in fall. Woolly Buggers (#6-12) and Patuxent Specials (#10-12) are also highly effective (see Chapter 13), the latter as an impressionistic crayfish imitation.

Last, but not least, are the midges. Gray and cream midges (#20-26), as well as black flies (#20) hatch throughout the year. When fish are rising and you just cannot see what they are taking, the chances are good that midges are at work. In Chapter 13 we describe an effective arsenal of midge patterns that can be fished top to bottom. These work on the Savage as well as any river with midging fish.

The River and Its Problems

The Savage River has numerous plusses for the fly angler. Within the context of the great diversity we have underscored, this year-round fishery contains a high density of wild trout that are strong and healthy, four different species of trout, the best hatches in the state, a wide variety of structure and holding water, and water quality and temperatures that provide a great environment for trout, insect life, and thus fishing. All of this occurs in a visually pleasing environment.

As we see it, this tailwater has no major problems, but it does have some limitations that need to be taken into account. Because of the quality of the angling, the river has gotten more fishing pressure of late. In fact, anglers travel significant distances to try their tactics on the Savage's often fussy trout. For example, on one nice January weekend day, 22 cars were counted along the river, with half of them being from out of state. Naturally, you will find less fishing traffic on weekdays. On the other hand, given the density of fish, along with the fact that fish can hold in virtually every part of the river, you will not need a big piece of water to yourself in order to work to a lot of trout. Indeed, we have found that it may take several hours to work a few hundred feet of water on the Savage. Pods of rising fish will surely slow you down, as will be the fact that each pocket, eddy, riffle, and run likely holds trout. The point: It is easy to find a piece of water, even in crowded conditions, that can produce satisfying fishing.

Another limitation pertains to the whitewater releases. Although the major releases do not occur during the summer, one never knows when the release will be of a magnitude that fishing is diminished or just not viable. Do call in advance to find out the water level and release that is in effect when you hope to fish. Again the number is 410-962-7687.

High gradient and very slippery rocks make for extremely tough wading, a third limitation to be kept in mind. Anglers need to pay attention to every step they take when wading the Savage. As we have noted, cleats and/or a wading staff are called for.

The Upper Savage

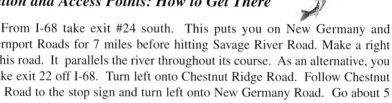

The Savage River above the reservoir offers a very different fishing situation. This put-and-take section has a five fish limit. It is stocked with rainbow trout of varying sizes, some in the "submarine" range. As with all put-and-take streams in the state, the river is quite crowded on the few days after each of the "opening days." Following these times, the crowds diminish significantly, and there are still fish left.

The hatching situation is similar to the lower river, although the hatches are not as prolific and occur a few weeks later. Generally, there is very good dry fly fishing in this section, although it does not have the quantity of fish present in the lower section. Although still tricky, the upper Savage is not as difficult to wade as the lower Savage. Naturally, since it is above the reservoir, one does not need to contend with the varying water levels due to releases. The water does get low during summer. We consider the upper Savage a good spring and early summer fishery after the opening day crowds have diminished.

Location and Access Points: How to Get There

From I-68 take exit #24 south. This puts you on New Germany and Westernport Roads for 7 miles before hitting Savage River Road. Make a right onto this road. It parallels the river throughout its course. As an alternative, you can take exit 22 off I-68. Turn left onto Chestnut Ridge Road. Follow Chestnut Ridge Road to the stop sign and turn left onto New Germany Road. Go about 5 miles and turn left onto Big Run Road, and continue until it dead ends at Savage River Road. Turn left to access the upper section, and turn right to get to the lower section. When going to the lower section, Savage River Road will run along the reservoir before the river appears.

The access points to the lower section are evident. Just look for parking pullovers. There are dirt roads of a few yards leading from Savage River Road to the pools at the two suspension bridges. Note that there are a few pieces of posted water along the river. These will be evident to you as you drive by.

CHAPTER 10
THE CASSELMAN RIVER
Spring Bonanza

T he Casselman River is one of the "big four" in western Maryland's Garrett County. Although it does not hold fish over the summer as the other three rivers in this county do, it is a pleasure to fish during certain parts of the year, as we shall discuss. Located in the heart of Amish farm country near the town of Grantsville, the drive to the river can be as charming as the river itself. The Casselman contains a very high density of trout during spring and again in fall. Due to stocking policies in recent years, the river has also held, on the average, some of the largest fish in the state.

The special regulation stretch of the Casselman covers approximately four and a half miles. It begins at the Interstate 68 bridge and continues downstream (north) to the Pennsylvania state line. This stretch meanders through farmland, but the water is lined with deciduous trees. Most of the river is on private property, and the landowners have been very receptive to angling. There are even signs stating that anglers are welcome. Of course, such receptivity can cool very quickly if anglers are not respectful of the property. Please take special care by not leaving trash, driving slowly on River Road, not trampling crops, etc.

Like the Youghiogheny River, the Casselman flows south to north. This fact makes these two rivers fishable when heavy rains muddy up the Savage or the North Branch of the Potomac, Garrett county's other premier rivers. The special reg stretch of the Casselman is managed as a delayed harvest water. Catch-and-release, flies and lures only, is in effect until June 16, at which point the regulation changes to two fish a day, with bait permitted. Then on October 1, the policy goes back to catch-and-release, flies and lures only.

Delayed harvest is the perfect regulation for the Casselman. In a typical year, the river has a nice flow and cool temperatures into early June. Then the flow drops precipitously and the water warms a great deal. By the end of June, the flow is usually at a trickle, and the temps are up into the 80s. During heat spells, they can even reach 90 degrees. What happens is that as the flows drop during early summer, the rocks become exposed and heat up greatly. In turn, these heated rocks warm the water.

As the river warms, fish that survive seek the cooling water provided by the five springheads on the special regulation stretch. Where little, cool feeders enter the stream, we have witnessed the phenomenon of trout stacked like cordwood in a few square feet, struggling for oxygen.

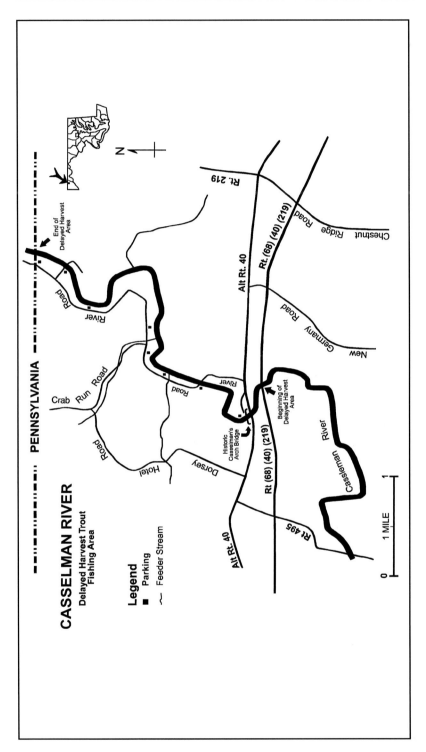

PENNSYLVANIA

CASSELMAN RIVER

Delayed Harvest Trout
Fishing Area

Legend
■ Parking
⌢ Feeder Stream

End of
Delayed Harvest
Area

N

Rt. 219

Rt (68) (40) (219)

Chestnut Ridge Road

Alt Rt. 40

New Germany Road

River Road

Crab Run Road

Road

River

Hotel Road

Dorsey Road

Rt (68) (40) (219)

Beginning of
Delayed Harvest
Area

Historic
Casselman's
Arch Bridge

Casselman River

Rt 495

Alt Rt. 40

0   1 MILE   1

The Casselman is a low gradient river that is generally 40 to 60' wide. Its bottom is lined with rocks and pebbles. There are many small riffles and runs that hold fish, as well as a few large pools. These pools generally are visible from the several pullovers that will be evident as you drive along River Road. Between the pools and productive riffles/runs, there are stretches of shallow water that tends to hold few fish. Spring flows can be heavy. You can check the gauge at the River Road Bridge, which you will cross within a mile of Route 68. Levels of 1.8' to 2.2' are the best for fishing. Flows above 3.5 make things pretty difficult.

The Fish and the Fishing

Rainbow and brown trout are stocked in the Casselman in good numbers. For example, Ken Pavol, who is the manager of the DNR's freshwater fisheries program for the western part of the state, reports that typically over 8000 trout are stocked per year in the Casselman. That's a lot of fish for 4-1/2 miles of water. If flows and temperatures permit, trout are stocked in the fall as well as in the spring. As is characteristic of all special regulation waters in Maryland, there is no closed season on the Casselman.

In recent years, the Casselman has gotten the reputation for being a big fish river. When Garrett County guide, Keith Albright, gives his slide show on the western Maryland streams, he displays several slides of true submarines (in the 3-4 lb. range) that were caught on this water. Is Keith's experience an anomaly? Is the big fish reputation of the Casselman deserved? In an interview with Ken Pavol, he noted that the Cassleman is earmarked as a big fish river, and the DNR does stock several hundred big fish in this stretch of water each year. The Casselman's reputation is indeed earned.

As far as fishing the Casselman is concerned, a few points are worth noting. First, as Albright points out, it is best to fish this river while standing on or near the banks. This is so because many fish hold close to the banks, and if you just wade into the river, you will spook them. Keith tells the story of an angler fishing choice water near the new River Road bridge and getting skunked. The angler, however, was wading in some of the best channels in that section. After the angler left, and a few minutes were allowed for the water and the fish to "calm down," Keith and his fishing buddies caught and released several heavy trout from the exact spot where the earlier angler had stood.

In late winter and early spring, streamers and other attractor patterns are the ticket (see next section on hatches and patterns). Then, as the stocked fish acclimate, and spring hatches intensify in May, nymphs and dry flies work well. Although dry fly activity tends to be best in late May and early June, surface activity can occur much earlier, and it is wise to be observant. For example, Charlie recalls his first experience on the Casselman several seasons ago. On a late April morning, about 11 AM, Charlie approached a nice pool in the middle section of the special reg water. A spin fisherman was just leaving after not having caught fish. Charlie tried a streamer for several minutes without any results. As he was getting

One of the many historic scenes one can experience on a fishing excursion in Maryland.

ready to leave and wondering if there were any fish in this pool, rises began to occur, even though hatches were not in evidence. In the next half hour, several very nice trout were taken on the Simple Three Hackle, a great all-around surface pattern (size #18 and 20; see Chapter 13 for recipe). Then Charlie moved to the lower bridge pool, and took several more fish on this same pattern. When larger surface patterns were tried, however (including Three Hackles), only refusals occurred.

Regarding tackle, the Casselman fishes well with fly rods in the 8-9' range, with line weights being determined by the kind of fishing you are doing. Anywhere from 2-6 weights are fine, but the heavier weights make for easier casting if you are slinging weighted flies. Leaders of any length will work, although we prefer 7 1/2' ones, tapered to 4X. Tippets of 4X or 5X are usually just fine. If you are fishing flies that are size #18 or below, however, 6X is a good idea. While hip waders are all you need on this river, there may be a few instances where chest waders will give you a small advantage. We always recommend a good pair of polarized lenses. At the same time, rather than sight fishing on the Casselman, you fish to likely holding areas, and of course to rises when they occur.

On the whole, the Casselman is a comfortable river to fish. It is a very open river, and this makes the casting very easy. The little wading you need to do is also easy. The fish tend to be agreeable, and when they are feeding, they are catchable

Spring flows on the Casselman River.

if good presentations are made with a reasonable pattern. As always, fish that are caught and released several times do get "educated," so effective tactics and techniques are essential.

Hatching, Other Stream Life, and Effective Patterns

Hatching on the Casselman is not spectacular, but there is usually enough hatching to keep the fish active. As is usual in Maryland waters, the tiny black winter stonefly (#18) from January through March, followed by the brown stonefly (#14-16) in March, usher in the year. There are small quill Gordons (#12-14) and Hendricksons (#10-12, including the male red quill, #14) hatches in April. The blue-winged olive (#16-20) peaks in April, but emerges on cloudy days during much of the spring. A few March browns (#10) and green drakes (#8-10) hatch in May, and light cahills (#14) are in evidence especially in June.

As far as mayflies are concerned, the best hatch on the Casselman is the sulphur (#14-18) hatch. This hatch begins in earnest toward the end of May, so there are only a few weeks that it can be fished before the two trout per day regulation takes over. When that happens, there are many bait fisherman on the river, and the bigger fish tend to be taken out. Up to that point, though, fishing the sulphur hatch on the Casselman can be a blast!

A summer drought dehydrates the Casselman River to low, lows.

There are also some caddis hatches on the river, with tan caddis (#14-16) being the first to hatch, followed by olive-bodied and gray-bodied caddis (#14-16). Terrestrials such as ants, hoppers, and beetles are summer fare, but because the Casselman essentially dries up during most summers, this is not a good terrestrial situation. If the flows increase in Autumn, and when the water temperature falls, Crickets (#10-12) will take fish.

Regarding effective surface patterns, your favorite imitations of the mayflies we have noted will be effective, as will Elk or Deer Hair Caddis. The Three Hackle (#12-20) is an effective all-around surface pattern on the Casselman, as is the Adams (#12-20). The best size will of course depend on what is hatching at the time you are fishing, but, in general, a #16 of either of these patterns is perhaps the best choice.

As far as nymphs, any of a range of nymphs will work well, with size 14-18 Pheasant Tails and Gold-Ribbed Hare's Ears being our favorites because they "pick up" so many of the mayflies that hatch on most rivers. Try these with and without bead heads. Also try caddis larva and pupa, with and without bead heads.

Because some of the best fishing on the Casselman occurs in March and April, when there are not hot hatches, we think streamer fishing is often the ticket on this river. This is so especially for the submarines that inhabit its waters. Fluorescent Woolly Buggers and Patuxent Specials (#8-12; see Chapter 13) are our favorites, but a range of streamer patterns can be used, e.g., Sculpins (#6-10),

Muddler Minnows (#6-10), and crayfish imitations. Egg patterns (#8-10; especially with white glo bug yarn tied in behind the hook eye and draped over the egg) and Red San Juan Worms (#12-16) are also good choices.

The River and Its Problems

The Casselman River is an excellent spring fishery that holds many fish, and many very *big* fish. It fishes its best before the other major rivers of western Maryland are in their peak. It is also a good fall river, when the fall flows are high enough. When they are, you also have the advantage of beautiful fall foliage in the middle of Amish farm country. The river has the advantage of easy access, and its openness makes it also easy to cast and fish.

The Casselman's disadvantages are similar to those of all delayed harvest streams in the state. That is, the water gets too warm and low in summer to support trout. In particularly dry years, fall water levels are also too low for trout.

Because of the number and size of the fish, the Casselman now gets fairly heavy pressure in the spring, its prime season. Because of this, weekdays are best in the spring. Even when the fishing traffic is heavy, though, you can still find open areas with plenty of fish.

Location and Access Points

The Casselman is readily accessible, since River Road parallels it through-out the delayed harvest stretch. There are obvious pullovers, and usually good pools are near them.

To get to the Casselman from Interstate 68, take the Grantsville exit (#19). Go to the town of Grantsville and turn right onto Route 40. Continue on 40 until it crosses the river and in a few yards it runs by River Road. Make a left onto River Road, and in a short distance it crosses the river and then parallels it throughout the rest of the delayed harvest stretch. You can fish upstream of the River Road Bridge for a short distance, but the main fishing will occur from this bridge downstream.

CHAPTER 11

THE YOUGHIOGHENY RIVER

Sipping Fish in Big Waters

T he Youghiogheny River (pronounced yock-a-gainey) is one of Garrett County's "big four." It is also Maryland's largest trout stream. Flowing from south to north, like the Casselman, the Yock, as it is usually referred to, contains a four and a half mile catch-and-release section (artificial flies and lures only), which will be the focus of this chapter. In this stretch, the river ranges from about 80-180' in width, averaging approximately 100'. The sense of expansiveness created by the Yock is similar to that experienced on your big rivers out west. When wading this water, you will have a panoramic view of the big river and its heavily forested and mountainous banks as you look either up or down stream. Catch a sunset or a sunrise on the river, and you'll think you have gone to heaven. To those of us who cut our fly fishing teeth on tiny eastern streams and brooks, simply gazing at the Yock is quite an experience. As we shall see, fishing these big waters is even more interesting.

Because of the size of this river, the angler has a sense of openness and space. Even when other anglers are on the water, the bigness allows for a feeling of privacy. One rarely feels crowded on the Yock.

The Yock has lots of interesting structure. Its gradient is moderate, as is its flow. Boulders and cobbles, resembling varying sized bowling balls, line the bottom. There are also many flat, cut rocks that form deep channels or slots, and fish tend to line up in these channels. There are many long runs interspersed with relatively shallow riffles and deep pools. River depth varies from spot to spot, and also according to whether water is being released from the Deep Creek Lake discharge (see below). Under normal conditions (when water is not being released), the depth can range from a foot or so in the riffles to over 10 feet in the deepest pools. Although the flow is moderate on the average, it can be quite heavy, e.g., in the spring.

The Yock has been referred to as a hybrid tailwater. It receives a hydropower discharge from nearby Deep Creek Lake on an intermittent basis. This discharge is very central to the life of the fishery and to the way fishing and wading are to be approached. In the old days, before the discharge, the Yock was a scenic river that was devoid of trout after summer weather set in. Now fish can survive, even thrive, in the Yock year-round. The water release turned a marginal fishery into an excellent one. It helps cool the water in summer and warm it during cold western Maryland winters. The latter prevents freezing, which of course can be deadly to fish.

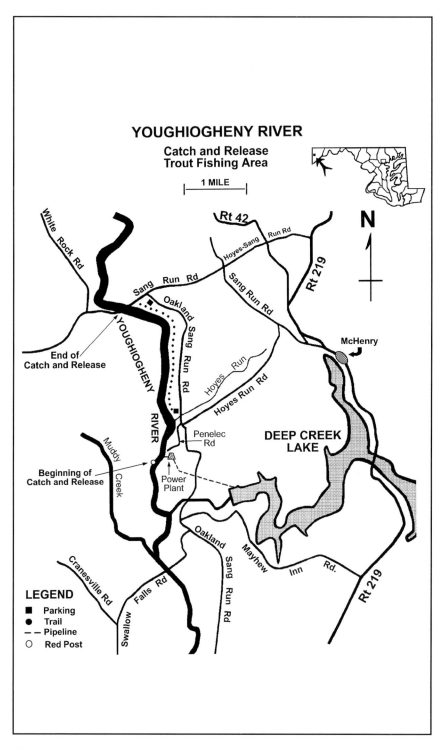

YOUGHIOGHENY RIVER

Catch and Release
Trout Fishing Area

1 MILE

N

White Rock Rd

Rt 42

Hoyes-Sang Run Rd

Sang Run Rd

Oakland Sang Run Rd

Rt 219

YOUGHIOGHENY RIVER

End of
Catch and Release

McHenry

Hoyes Run

Hoyes Run Rd

Penelec
Rd

DEEP CREEK
LAKE

Muddy Creek

Beginning of
Catch and Release

Power
Plant

Cranesville Rd

Swallow Falls Rd

Oakland Sang Run Rd

Mayhew Inn Rd.

Rt 219

LEGEND
■ Parking
● Trail
– – Pipeline
○ Red Post

Although there are no hard and fast rules about when or how much water is to be released, some general patterns do exist. For example, during your typical summer and fall conditions, releases occur on Mondays and Fridays, from about 10 AM to 1 PM. The amount of water released, however, will depend on the temperature and flow on the river. When the water gets above 75 degrees, the release (i.e., the cubic feet per second that is released) is increased. It will also be increased when the river is low. Depending on how much water is released, the water level may raise from about half a foot to two feet because of the discharge. This will have a great impact on how you fish the river, which will be discussed in the next section. For now, suffice it to say that the angler must pay close attention to the flow, and when the water begins rising, it is important that you cross to the side on which you are parked. Do so quickly, for you only have 5-10 minutes before the water rises. Note that no whistles or horns will warn you of the rise, although you can actually hear the water moving faster. For information on water releases, you can call 814-533-8911. If you forget to bring this book with you, the phone number is given on a kiosk at the Hoyes Run parking area.

In normal conditions, the Yock is wadable. Although there are deep pools, you can usually find areas where the river can be waded and even crossed. The rocks are not nearly as slippery as those on the Savage or North Branch of the Potomac, but the wading can still be very tough. That is because of the shapes of the rocks never seem to permit your wading shoes to land in a comfortable position.

On the east side of the river, a trail parallels most of the catch-and-release section and connects to the parking lots on both the upper and lower parts of this section. On the portion upstream of the Hoyes Run parking lot (see Location and Access Points), a road runs along the river. Regarding the trail that parallels the river, it moves a fair distance from the river, and often you will need to climb down banks to access the river from the trail. But in many spots, the banks are not too steep and the trail not too far from the river. What this translates into is that the river is quite accessible, in terms of wading as well as places from which to enter it.

The Fish and the Fishing

No adult trout are stocked on the Yock. Fingerling rainbow and brown trout are stocked, and the strain of rainbow that is stocked is unusually adaptable to warmer water than is ideal for most salmonids. Because they were stocked as fingerlings, trout in this river have all the desirable characteristics of streambred fish. They are healthy, strong, and wise enough to make the fishing interesting.

Just a few years ago, the Yock actually had too many trout. This seemed to keep the average size smaller than was interesting for most anglers. It seemed like there were just too many 7-9" fish. The numbers have diminished in recent years, though, and the size has gone up proportionately. Currently the average trout is about 10-12", with some being 15" or above. While this is still not a big fish river, there is now a high density of healthy, strong, and "big enough" fish.

A wide range of subsurface patterns are effective on the Yock. However, the feature that to our mind distinguishes this fishery is the extent to which fish feed on the surface. For the angler who loves to fish dry flies, and also enjoys fishing tiny patterns (see next section on hatches and patterns), the Yock can be fly fishing nirvana. Especially in the upper reaches of the catch-and-release section, above the Hoyes Run parking area, there always seem to be rising fish. Many of them sit near the surface and gently but consistently sip the abundant insect life floating by. Beware, though, these are challenging fish to catch!

Although you can find fish anywhere, it is often most effective to fish the deep channels that are apparent. These channels tend to hold the most fish. Also, it is helpful to change flies a lot, as the fish seem to acclimate to patterns quickly. If you don't change flies, you should change locations. This is so because the fish habituate to a pattern, and once they do, it is very unlikely that they will inhale it.

When the water warms in the dead of summer, the fish tend to move to the upper portion of the catch-and-release section because the water there is cooler. The water from the Hoyes Run parking area up the coldwater discharge is by far the most effective under these summer conditions.

Regarding tackle, rods between 8-1/2' and 9-1/2' are best on this big water, with good line weights ranging from 3-6. Floating line is clearly preferred, given the surface activity that you are likely to encounter. If there is an ideal outfit for the Yock, we would say it is a 9' for 4 wt. rod that is soft enough that you will not break off light tippets when you strike sipping fish. The longer rods are preferred on the Yock because longer casts are often necessary on this big water to reach rising or nymphing fish. The up side of such a situation is that the openness of the river permits long casting. This is perhaps Maryland's best river in terms of allowing the fly angler to haul off and shoot long casts without worrying about getting snagged on overhangs.

If fishing on the surface, we recommend 9-12' leaders tapered to 4X or 5X, with 2-3' tippets. Depending on the size of patterns you use, tippets can range from 5X to 7X. When fishing to sipping fish with small flies (#20 and smaller) in low summer flows, we like 7X. If fishing underneath, shorter tippets (1-2'), with diameters between 4X and 6X will work fine.

Longer leaders and tippets for surface fishing on the Yock are desirable because of the complex currents common to this river. Drag becomes an ever present issue, and longer leaders and tippets are one of the ways to combat that. Of course, proper line control through mending and reach casting are also very important.

Although long casts can be made on the Yock, it is a good idea to get as close to rising fish as possible (without spooking them). Because the complex currents put many S's and curves in your line as it rides the surface, long distance casting on the Yock is often not very productive. When the fish does strike the fly, all those S's and curves makes it seem like your strike takes forever to get telegraphed to the fish. A solid hookup under such conditions is not a high percentage event. This problem is solved if you can inch closer, e.g., within 40' of the fish.

The Yock's width provides a lot of room for both trout and anglers.

You definitely should wear chest waders on the Yock, and your wading shoes should have felt soles. Because the rocks are hard to negotiate, as we have said, a wading staff on this river will be advantageous. You may get by without it, but it will make your life a whole lot easier!

We have mentioned the fact that the cold water hydropower discharge from Deep Creek Lake significantly affects fishing on the Yock. We discussed this situation with Don Hershfeld, who owns the Bed & Breakfast called Streams and Dreams adjacent to the Hoyes Run parking area and who studies and fishes the Yock intensively. Don explains how you can "play hop-scotch with the release," and thus not lose fishing time. If you have called the number we have given and found out that a release is planned, you can start the day at the lower parking area (adjacent to the Sang Run lot) and fish there until the released water gets to this section. Since releases usually begin about 10 AM, runs for about three hours, and take about 1.5 hours to reach the lower section, you can take a lunch break when the "high tide" hits this lower section, and then drive up to the upper parking lot (the Hoyes Run lot) and begin fishing in early afternoon. Fishing is often dynamite after the released water has moved through this upper section. Our theory as to why fishing can be so productive after the cold water passes through is this: The cold water serves to energize the trout. Then, when it recedes, the water warms a few degrees, which triggers insect hatching. This hatching naturally stimulates feeding by the trout, who had already been energized by the colder water.

Hatches, Other Stream Life, and Effective Patterns

Like most of the state's waters, the Yock has no spectacular individual hatches. But this river has plenty of insect life, including a wide range of very good hatches. It also has a good supply of baitfish. In fact, there always seems to be something hatching. For instance, when fishing the Yock during a late October evening, caddises, flying ants, midges, and small olive spinners were observed. On a warm January day, one of our fishing buddies, Rick Banvard, reported a nice hatch of blue-winged olives. Rick observed many rising fish, and he caught many, too. In the middle of a July heat wave, many rising fish were found throughout the late afternoon and evening.

The most significant mayfly, caddis, and stonefly hatches on the Yock are very similar to those on the Savage River, although hatches on the Yock typically occur a week or two earlier and are not quite as intense and diverse. We refer you to the hatch information in Chapter 9 (Savage River), and here we shall note some of the distinguishing features of hatching on the Yock. Although there is a wide range of hatching on this river, a few hatches stand out. First, the blue-winged olive is perhaps the river's best hatch. A larger olive (#16) appears in April and then smaller ones (#18-24) peak in July through September. However, you can see olive hatches from about April through winter. Look for olive spinner falls, also, especially on summer evenings.

There is now a fishable green drake (#8-10) hatch from late May into early June. When fish key in on these huge flies, they seem to throw their usual caution to the wind. There are sulphurs (#14-20) appearing from late May into July, and light cahills (#14) hatch from early June into August. These are not nearly as prolific as they are on the Savage, but they are just enough to get trout going.

Mayfly patterns approximating the hatches given above will take fish at the appropriate times. The Adams (#16-22), which is said to imitate everything and nothing, is also an effective pattern for the blue-winged olive hatch, since so many of these "olives" have medium to dark gray bodies. Be sure to have some emerger patterns for any mayfly hatch, since fish will at times take these when they refuse the duns.

An assortment of caddises (#14-18; olive, tan, and gray bodied) appears on the Yock from about April into late fall. In fact, the caddis in general is one of the best hatches on this river. In his writing and presentations, western Maryland guide Keith Albright notes that his favorite pattern is a Slate-Gray Elk Hair Caddis (gray wings and body, and grizzly hackle palmered through the body), with #16 being his favorite size. Olive and tan bodied Elk Hair Caddis (#14-18) are also terrific fish takers. To this list, Keith adds an unusual pattern that is highly effective on the Yock. Try Cream Moth patterns (#6-8) in the AM from late spring into fall.

Midges (#20-26) are ever-present (gray, black, and cream being the most prominent), and are often what those tough sippers are inhaling. A range of midges work well (see the patterns in Chapter 13), but in our experience the Griffiths Gnat

A warning of a peril on the Yock.

(#20-24) is the best surface midge pattern. A close second is the Three Hackle (#20-22, see Chapter 13), perhaps because it resembles various microcaddis that appear on the Yock. At times when fish are feeding on the itsy-bitsies, an angler can pick off one fish after another by alternating these two patterns.

The Yock is an excellent terrestrial river. Beetles (#14-18) and black ants (#16-22, including flying ants) are plentiful in the summer months. Fish beetle and ant patterns under the trees that line the river's banks, and especially under branches that extend several feet over the water. And during the dead of summer, grasshoppers (#8-12) become candy for the trout feeding near banks. Just slap hoppers on the water and twitch them. Fish will often first bump the hopper pattern, and then gulp it. Don't strike too quickly.

There is a little bit of everything for the angler who prefers fishing underneath the surface. Assorted beadhead nymphs (Prince Nymphs, Gold-Ribbed Hare's Ears, Pheasant Tails, caddis, soft-hackles) all take fish very effectively. Also, a range of streamer patterns fished down and across can pick up some larger fish. Woolly Buggers, Muddler Minnows, Marabou Muddlers, Clouser Minnows, Patuxent Specials, and Sculpin patterns all work very well.

The River and Its Problems

The Yock is big scenic river containing a high density of fish. There is some reproduction, but most of the trout are stocked as fingerlings. Thus, for all intents and purposes, these are wild fish that behave like wild fish. There is an abundance of insect life and baitfish in the river, so the trout have plenty to eat. The river is easy to access, is ordinarily wadable, and is very open. The latter permits easy casting. The river provides year-round fishing, and some of the very best dry fly fishing in the state.

There are some problems, though, that are worth noting. Anchor ice (ice forming on the river's bottom) occurring during winter limits reproduction. The lower portion of the catch-and-release stretch is essentially a long riffle and does not contain much structure. Lack of much structure, along with warming water, cause the fish to move upstream, as we have mentioned, in the hot days of summer. At those times, the fish are thus not as well dispersed as one would like.

Although not what we consider a problem, the rising water due to hydro-power discharges is an issue that the angler must continually be aware of. To our mind, this discharge has saved the Yock. At the same time, it creates a situation in which angler caution and awareness are very important.

Location and Access Points: How to Get There

To get to the catch-and-release stretch, take I-68 to exit #14A, which is Route 219, south. Stay on Route 219 for about 11 miles to the town of McHenry. Turn right at the Citgo gas station onto Sang Run Road and drive for about a half mile to Hoyes Run Road. Make a left onto Hoyes Run Road and continue for three miles to its end at a stop sign. Make a right onto Oakland-Sang Run Road, and proceed 0.1 miles to the upper parking area on the left, just across a small bridge. There is room for 6-7 cars here. A map on the bulletin board at that lot shows the access trail along the river.

To get to the lower portion of the catch-and-release stretch, continue on Oakland-Sang Run Road for about three and a half miles to a stop sign. Turn left onto Sang Run Road and go 0.1 miles to a large parking area immediately off the river.

As we have said, a trail covers the entire river between Hoyes and Sang Run Roads. And, above Hoyes Run Road, a paved access road (Penelec Road) parallels the river all the way to the coldwater discharge area.

CHAPTER 12
NORTH BRANCH OF THE POTOMAC RIVER
A River Reborn

I t seems fitting that the final river we explore in this book is the North Branch of the Potomac. This is because in many ways the North Branch epitomizes the positive developments that have occurred in Maryland trout fishing in recent times. After years of being essentially a dead river, the North Branch is just now beginning to come into its own. A quote by Ed Russell provides a sad picture of what for years had been the North Branch's plight:

> "For nearly 100 years Maryland's North Branch of the Potomac River was devoid of life — lifeless. No fish. No insects. Not even plants could live in the river's cold crystalline waters. The river's beautiful glides, imposing rapids, and deep mysterious pools seemed full of promise, but they were empty of substance" (*Fly Fisherman*, May 1996, p. 65).

What caused this tragic situation? In a more positive vein, what has changed to bring this river back to life? Before answering these questions, a bit of background is in order. The North Branch has become one of the big four rivers of Garrett County. Throughout its reaches, it forms the border between Maryland and West Virginia, and now contains more than 20 miles of fishable trout water. This fishable water includes 13 miles of river under special regulations, which makes it the longest special reg stretch in the state. The North Branch has two distinct sections that almost seem like two different rivers: The section upriver of the Jennings-Randolph Reservoir, and the section below the reservoir. We shall talk about both of these sections in this chapter.

Now back to our questions of what killed the river and what has brought it back to life. Answers to the first question are straightforward. Acid runoff from coal mining operations conducted many decades ago wiped out nearly all living organisms in the North Branch. When coal miners dug into the earth, they naturally struck water. As this water spilled over the iron pyrites embedded in coal deposits, it produced sulfuric acid. When the acid-laced water poured into the nearest stream or river, it naturally annihilated everything in its course. The North Branch was not spared. Acid runoff still regularly occurs through abandoned mine shafts.

The rebirth of the North Branch, and all that went into it, is an immensely happier tale. It is also a testimony to what can happen with enlightened and creative resources management. In the solution, many forces came into play, the major ones being: An environmentally responsible mining operation spurred on by new mining laws; the building of devices that significantly reduce the acidity of the water; and the construction of the Jennings-Randolph Reservoir and dam. Let's briefly look at each of these remedies.

In the late 1970s, the Surface Mining Act required that mining companies straighten up their act and eliminate the acid runoff problem. The Mettiki Coal Company, which now owns nearly all of the coal mines in western Maryland, has been a model citizen. Acidic waters from mining operations, including abandoned shafts, are funnelled into huge underground basins. Through a complex pumping process, this water is then treated with limestone to neutralize the acid. Thus, by the time that this potentially deadly water flows into the North Branch, it is no longer acidic. This does not solve all of the river's problems, however, since there remains a substantial amount of damaging runoff from locations upriver of where the Mettiki Company is neutralizing the acid.

Another creative solution was needed and, in fact, has occurred. The Maryland Department of Environment has installed devices called *limestone dosers* (five of them) upstream of the reservoir. Originated in Sweden, these silo-like dosers pipe limestone into feeder streams on the upper North Branch (above the reservoir). The tons of limestone pumped into the river daily modify the water of the North Branch, including the water in the reservoir and the river below it. What once was a pH level of around 4 (similar to vinegar) has dramatically improved to approximately 7 — an excellent level for the organisms that inhabit a trout river.

The last change that resurrected the North Branch was the building of the Jennings-Randolph Dam in 1982. The dam contains five water intakes at varying depths. This allows for control of water temperature and flow in what is fast becoming a top tailwater fishery. Releases from the lower levels in summer, for example, permit cool waters, and in the winter prevent the water from becoming too frigid.

We should mention another potential solution to the acid runoff problem — a truly "low tech" solution — that is also being tried. Cattails are now being grown to supplement the effects of the limestone dosers. These plants have a neutralizing effect on acid runoff, and they are being grown in areas where such runoff is evident. It will be interesting to determine the long-term effect of the cattails.

Let's now look at the river and the fishing. Below we divide the North Branch into its two distinct sections. We first discuss the lower river, the tailwater that has gotten the greatest amount of attention recently. Then we take of look at the upper river (above the reservoir). Our focus will be on the special regulation waters in each section.

The Lower North Branch

Whenever we fish the North Branch, we feel awed by its size and its uniquely eastern beauty. This big water has been referred to as the Madison of the east.

One of the many deep pools on the North Branch where lunker trout reside.

Although we do not believe it is yet of that quality, its beauty is more striking than that of the legendary western river. Pushing its way through a valley, between two mountains, as it does, the river is big and brawling. Its generally green coloration creates the sense of an emerald carpet as the river often rushes, but sometimes glides, through its course.

Part of the river's beauty is the wildlife that you encounter during your fishing time. The North Branch does not disappoint, as it contains more wildlife than perhaps any river in the state. It is one of the few places where you may be joined by a big bear on the water, providing a different kind of thrill than a big trout.

As we have said, this is a big river. In places it is more than 150' wide, with an average of about 70-90'. The river is very open, so that fly casting is not a problem.

There are two catch-and-release sections (artificial flies and lures only) on the lower North Branch (see map). When you drive down to the river on Barnum Road (see Location and Access Points) to a clearly designated parking area, you will see old bridge abutments on the river. One catch-and-release section begins about 100 yards above these abutments. You will notice a cable crossing the river at the lower end of a long glide (that has lots of fish in it). This cable, along with a not-so-obvious red post on the opposite side of river, demarcates the beginning of the upper catch-and-release section. This section continues for about three-quarters of a mile *upstream*, where another cable crosses the river. This approximately one-

NORTH BRANCH POTOMAC RIVER
Catch and Release Trout Fishing Area

1 MILE

N

Rt. 36

Savage River

Rt. 135

Luke   WESTERNPORT

End of
Catch and Release

North Branch Potomac River

Piney Swamp Run

Rt. 46 (gravel road)

Beginning of
Catch and Release   Blue Hole

End of
Catch and Release

Upper
Bridge
Abutment

Barnum Road

Jennings Randolph Lake

Lynn Run

Beginning of
Catch and Release   Churches

LEGEND
•••• Trail
■ Parking
o Red Post
▬ Cable
+–+ Old Railroad Bed

mile stretch contains one very inviting piece of water after another. Above that, fishing is not permitted, as the state operates fish-rearing pens.

The downstream catch-and-release section begins below the Blue Hole and covers about four miles of choice water. The Blue Hole is one of the truly huge holes on the river, being probably 150' wide, 300' long, and very deep. The beginning of this catch-and-release section is again demarcated by a cable crossing the river, and a nonobvious red post on the far bank. The section ends at Piney Swamp Run, a little feeder stream that you are unlikely to find!

The mile or so stretch between the two catch-and-release sections (including the Blue Hole) is open water, with a 5-fish per day limit, and no tackle restrictions. Due to heavy stocking (by West Virginia, as well as Maryland) along with high quality habitat, this is one of the few pieces of open water in the state that will just not get fished out. If you have a good pair of polarized lenses, you can observe many fish in this stretch in the dead of summer, and few bait fishermen will be present.

In both the catch-and-release and the open water, you will encounter a wide variety of structural qualities. There are many riffles, runs, rapids, long pools and glides, cuts between rocks, and rock walls and ledges. In the lower catch-and-release section, you will even encounter a piece of water that resembles a staircase, as the water rolls over a series of steps.

The gradient of the North Branch is typically referred to as moderate. Don't let that fool you. This river carries a great push of water, and in many ways resembles a much higher gradient river. The flow in terms of cubic feet per second (cfs) is typically in the 250 to 500 range. A cfs between about 200 and 400 makes for the best fishing, whereas as it climbs above 450, it can be very difficult to negotiate the river. When the cfs rises to about 600, it is wise to fish one of the other good rivers that are nearby. Since flow is such an important factor, before you leave home to fish the North Branch, you should call 410-962-7687 for information on flow. This is especially important in April and May, when there are whitewater releases that can bring the cfs to 1000, great for whitewater rafting but perilous for wading. Releases can also occur during times other than these.

The river contains a rocky bottom, with the rocks resembling bowling balls of varying sizes. Some sections contain a good amount of gravel. We consider the North Branch to be the most difficult river in the state to wade (in the same league as the Savage, but even more difficult). Like so many tailwaters, the rocks always seem to be misplaced and misshapen, and your wading shoes never seem to land evenly on them. If this, along with the usually heavy push of water, were not enough, the fact that so many of the rocks are extremely slippery creates all the makings of treacherous wading situation. (The "greasy" rocks are a result of lime-stone treatment.) We think that anglers should use wading staffs on this river, and their felt soles should have cleats. If you do not bring a staff, find a good stick in the woods to help you out. Whatever aids you bring, be sure to wade carefully, taking one step at a time, and paying careful attention to where your wading shoes are landing.

Because it is a tailwater in which water can be released from the dam at varying levels, the river never warms up too much. It generally does not get more than a few degrees above 60, and in winter it tends to stay around 40 degrees, even during the very frigid western Maryland winters. This is a great situation for trout to flourish in. If the air temperature is tolerable, you can fish the North Branch well into winter. As the colder weather sets in, fish closer to the dam, for the water will be a few degrees warmer.

The Fish and the Fishing

You will find brown trout, rainbows, native brookies, and, yes, cutthroat trout in the North Branch. Thus, your best chance of a Maryland grand slam — all four species — exists on this river. Although some reproduction is now occurring, most of the fish you encounter will have been stocked by the state of Maryland, and some by West Virginia (other than the brookies). In fact, there are more fish stocked in the North Branch than any other river in Maryland. It should be noted, however, that no adult trout are stocked in the catch-and-release sections. Only fingerling browns, rainbows, and cutthroats are stocked. Because they are stocked as fingerlings, these fish have essentially all the fighting qualities and "wisdom" of streambred fish.

The existence of cutthroat trout in Maryland is a story in itself. In the late 1980s, Bob Bachman, who was then head of the state's Freshwater Fisheries Division, and a person who did as much as, or more than, anyone we know for Maryland trout fishing, originated the idea. For several years now, the state has been purchasing 50,000 or so fertilized eggs, which are then stocked as fingerlings. By all accounts, these cutthroats are doing well in the North Branch, exhibiting impressive growth rates, and actually reproducing occasionally. While only fingerlings are stocked in the catch-and-release waters, adult trout are put into the open water. The average fish is in the 11-12" range, but some of the stocked trout are hummers.

If clients we guide want to catch big fish *on the average*, we take them to Big Hunting Creek. If clients, on the other hand, want a few hummers in the spring, we suggest the Casselman. However, if these anglers wanted to shoot for record-level trout any time of the year, the North Branch is clearly the choice. In his slide show presentations, Western Maryland guide Keith Albright notes that his best big fish day on the North Branch was five trout over 20" — a spectacular day by any yardstick. Also note that the state records for brown trout, cutthroats, and brook trout are on this river. The record brown was over 12 lbs.!

Regarding fishing tackle, we like longer rods on this big river, 8-1/2' or preferably 9'. Line weights in the range of 3-7 are all appropriate, depending on what kinds of flies you are throwing at the trout. To our mind, if there is an ideal all around rod on the North Branch, it is a 9' for 5 wgt. A weight-forward line will give you a bit of an advantage when making long casts, as is sometimes needed on this river. We prefer floating lines in nearly all situations, although we should note

Here the North Branch gives the impression that it might be kin to a river out west.

that Albright at times prefers a 10' sink tip line to get down to where the big fish live. And he also uses big subsurface flies (e.g., #4 Clouser Minnows) when going for the submarines. Keith, by the way, refers to the North Branch as a "dredging river," because he likes to shoot for those submarines that lurk down deep.

When you fish the North Branch, leave your hip waders at home. This is a river for which chest waders are highly preferable, if not required. Be sure to keep the belt tight on your waders, for a spill is commonplace, and a tight belt prevents the waders from filling up with water. During colder months, neoprene waders are desirable. Three millimeter neoprenes are a good choice.

Although some view the North Branch as a "dredging river," the hatches have steadily improved (see Hatches, Other Stream Life, and Patterns), and the surface fishing can be quite good. When fishing on the surface, 9' to 12' leaders are desirable, with 2-3' tippets. Generally, tippets of 5X are fine, although you will want to move to 6X when using smaller flies (e.g., #18-20). For subsurface fishing, tippets of 3X-5X are usually best, again depending on the size of your patterns. If we are fishing standard #10-18 nymphs, 5X will do the trick. If you go to bigger streamers, 3X and 4X are the choice.

Fishing on the North Branch can range from difficult to very easy, and to an extent this depends on the water release. Jay Sheppard, who guides on and fishes the North Branch frequently, tells the story of taking a group to the North Branch when the water was coming down. In a short time, the cfs dropped from 1000 to 350. When the water dropped, it warmed a bit, and hatches began to occur. The fish turned on, and within the next 3-4 hours, six anglers averaged about 20 fish apiece. Larry also recalls a day when the water dropped to 250 cfs. Cutthroats began feeding voraciously and Larry didn't bother to count how many were taken on fluorescent Woolly Buggers (see Chapter 13). A 3-1/2 pounder, however, was in this large group!

Hatches, Other Stream Life, and Effective Patterns

A typical comment on North Branch hatches is that they are poor but getting better. As of this writing, our judgment is that, although not remarkable, hatches are actually good and getting better. The improvement has been steady in the last few years, especially since the floods of 1996. According to Ken Pavol, the DNR's Western Regional Manager, big floods, such as occurred then, produce too much nitrogen below the dam. This tends to kill smaller fish and insects, and at least portions of the river are back to ground zero in terms of insect life. Thankfully, no big floods have occurred since 1996.

Since the hatch situation is in flux, we cannot be as specific and decisive as with other streams. However, at least some solid information is available. As in so many Maryland streams, the earliest hatches are stoneflies, especially the tiny black winter stonefly (#16-20) during the first three months of the year, and the bigger brown stonefly (actually dark brown, #14), in March and April. These represent good hatches, and they can be seen especially on warmer, sunny days.

Mayfly hatches are at this point variable. The "April grays" (blue quill, #18; quill Gordon, #12-14; Hendrickson, #10) appear, but not in notable numbers. Recently, a good March brown (#10-12) hatch has occurred in late May and June. Sulphurs (#14-18), which represent major hatches on the nearby Savage River, yield only a fair hatch on the North Branch. However, at this point there is a good light cahill hatch in the evenings from June into August. Also, there now appears to be very good blue-winged olive hatches from about April through the fall. Since these *Baetis* represent several different species, you will find them in widely differing sizes, ranging from as large as #14 to as small as #24. Keep your eyes out for mayflies that look gray as they peel off the water. (They have dark gray wings, and bodies ranging from dark gray to dark olive.) Hatches will be especially evident on cloudy days. These flies rarely pour off the water in large quantities on the North Branch. But if you see a few of them, and also notice fish dimpling the surface, try an olive pattern. An #18 is a good bet.

Imitative patterns of the same names as the insects noted above will work. Also try the Simple Three Hackle (#14-20; see Chapter 13 for recipe) when any of the April grays are on the water, and especially when blue-winged olives are at work.

The usual array of nymphs all work on the North Branch. Our favorites are Charlie's Nymph (#16-18) for the early stonefly hatches; Gold-Ribbed Hare's Ears (#12-16) and Pheasant Tails (#12-18) for virtually any of the mayfly hatches; and lighter colored March Brown nymphs (amber colored body and thorax; #10-12) when March browns are hatching. Bead head nymphs of the same names as above are excellent choices on the heavy waters of the Potomac. The beads help get your flies down fast, and their shiny appearance also helps get trouts' attention.

Caddis hatches are beginning to develop on the North Branch, with a wide range of these insects now evident. There is a little black sedge (#18) hatch in April, and caddises with tan, olive, and grayish bodies all follow. Although we have not seen it ourselves, we have heard reports of *Hydropsyches* (caddis with a cinnamon body and brown mottled wings, #16) hatching in fishable numbers in autumn. Elk Hair Caddis of the appropriate size and color are excellent choices on this river. You will likely not need more realistic patterns than the Elk Hair. Caddis larva, pupa, and soft hackles, especially with bead heads, are excellent fish takers.

There is good terrestrial fishing on the North Branch in the summer, especially Ants (#14-18), Beetles (#14-16), Crickets (#8-12), and sunken Inch-worms (#12-14). The Beetles, Ants, and Crickets are especially good in black, whereas the Inchworm is tied with chartreuse vernille.

We should note that big attractor patterns are especially good in the big and brawling sections that you will encounter. Wulff patterns (#8-14) and Humpies (#10-14) of various colors can be dynamite. Interestingly, the lower North Branch also has a good number of scuds (freshwater "shrimp", #16-18) and even cress bugs (#14-18). These are insects you typically find in limestone streams, so their appearance in the North Branch is very significant.

Finally, a really good baitfish population exists on the river. There are very good numbers of daces, sculpins, darters, and crayfish. A range of streamers will take fish, especially the larger fish. Our favorites are various colors of Clouser Minnows (#4-8), Woolly Buggers (#6-12), and Patuxent Specials (#8-12, see Chapter 13).

The Upper North Branch

Much of what we have said about the Lower North Branch applies to the upper section: Big water, beautiful surroundings, similar hatches. However, running through the Potomac State Forest, this upper section is even more remote. The few roads you will see are unpaved. In fact, one of the feeder streams to the upper section is called Lostland Run, a fitting name for this out-of-the-way place. The upper North Branch has been described as "wild and woolly." The gradient is high, the water fast and rugged. You will encounter rapids, deep pools, and rock ledges. The bottom is often bedrock, with lots of bedrock tables. Although it does not have the uneven rock structure of a tailwater, the wading can still be treacherous due to slippery rocks. When you fish this section, do not fish it alone. Have at least one companion, and don't get too far from each other.

Like the lower section, there are two sets of regulations. For about the first six miles upstream of the Jennings-Randolph Reservoir, there is a 5-fish limit, with no tackle restrictions. Then, near the point where Lostland Run enters the river, a delayed harvest policy kicks in and continues for about 7-8 miles upriver to the upper boundary of the Potomac State Forest, at Wallman. As usual in Maryland,

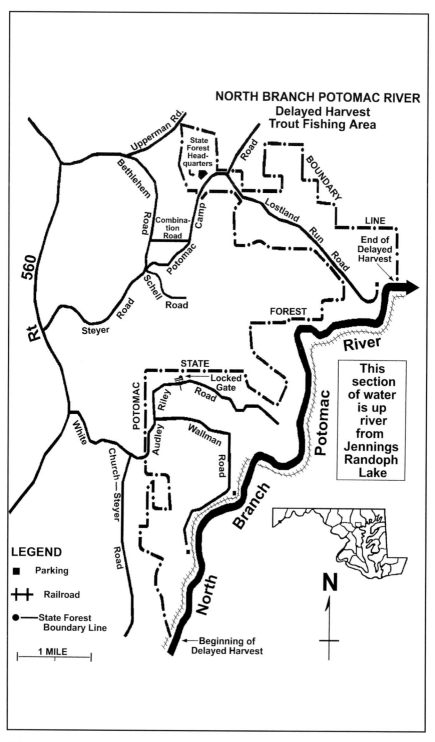

Low water exposing the many minature boulders in the North Branch Delayed Harvest Area giving an angler a visual map of where trout will hold in higher water flow.

delayed harvest means no fish can be kept from January 1 to June 15, and only artificial lures and flies are permitted. From June 16 through the last day of September, the creel limit is two per day, with no tackle restrictions. Then on October 1, the no-kill (flies and lures only) regulations return and continue to the next June. As has become customary, fish (usually rainbow trout) are again stocked in the delayed harvest section after October 1.

Above the delayed harvest section, the regs shift back to a 5-fish creel limit. This put-and-take stretch continues upstream for eight more miles, to the old Wilson Road bridge, and Sand Run.

The state stocks mostly adult rainbow trout in the upper section, and some of them are true lunkers. The best times to fish the upper North Branch are from about mid-March to mid-June. Although the amount of water is quite enough to hold fish through the summer, the water does warm from around mid June on. At the same time, feeder streams with cool water contain native brook trout, and also some rainbows. These rainbows can also be seen in the river right below the feeders; and when the water is warmest, you can find them bunched up near spring seeps.

Given the times of the year when the fishing is best on the upper North Branch, we especially recommend big underwater patterns, such as Clouser Minnows (#4-8), Woolly Buggers (#6-10), and Patuxent Specials (#8-10). Also, attractor dry flies as noted in the lower North Branch section are highly effective. If you nymph fish, do so after the freshly stocked fish have acclimated to the stream and the hatches, beginning in about April.

The River and Its Problems

The North Branch of the Potomac is fast developing into a premiere trout fishery. As the hatches continue to improve, it should eventually compare favorably to the top rivers in the region. It contains many fish, big fish, fish that are essentially wild (stocked as fingerlings), four species of trout — and all of this in the context of breathtakingly beautiful surroundings. Right now, the tailwater fishery is the best water for fly anglers. It has the best hatches, water temps that are near ideal for trout and insect life, and the greatest numbers of trout. Yet the upper river is also top-notch, especially before the hottest days of summer and again in the fall.

The river does have some problems worth mentioning. Since acid runoff from abandoned mines is not going to go away, the use of limestone dosers will continue to be needed in the foreseeable future. If the dosers break down for periods of time, there would be adverse effects. At this point, we do not yet know how pervasive will be the effects of the "low tech" solution — the cattails that are being planted where acid runoff occurs.

Although the hatches are developing nicely, the big water releases which are usually caused by large storms and which insert too much nitrogen in the water, are still a problem, since they adversely affect small fish and insect life. Major flooding would have very serious effects, so we can only hope that ways of preventing excessive nitrogen are developed. In a similar vein, it is important that you stay aware of water releases, and calling in advance of a trip is your best bet. Again, the number to call is 410-962-7687.

The very remoteness that makes the North Branch so desirable might also be considered something of a limitation. The upper section, in particular, is hard to get to, and the paths are irregular. In the sum of things, however, its remoteness is a prized commodity, and a rare one, too, in modern Maryland. Again, though, we do recommend fishing with a friend, especially in the upper river, but also in the tailwater.

Finally, there is the wading. Ironically, to an extent the wading problem has been caused by the remedy to a larger problem. The influx of limestone, which in many ways has saved the river, causes the rocks to become excessively slippery. All we can do is reiterate the need to walk carefully, and take along helpful supports such as a staff and cleats. You can probably do okay without the supports, but they will make the wading more viable, and less tedious.

One of the several lime dosers that have subdued acid runoff and revived the North Branch.

Location and Access Points: How to Get There

To the lower North Branch: For starters, remember that the lower North Branch can be accessed only from the West Virginia side, specifically from the town of Barnum. There is a shorter but harder way, and a longer but easier way, to get to the catch-and-release sections. Shorter and harder first: From I-68, take exit 34, which is Route 36, south. Take Route 36 to the town of Westernport. In Westernport, turn right (west) onto Route 135. Go about two miles to the Westvaco Paper Company and take a left to cross the river into West Virginia. Here you will pick up Route 46, which becomes a gravel road. Go about 3-1/2 miles to the first right (unmarked, but still Route 46). Go a mile to the second church on your left and make another right. (Note that all your turns have been rights.) This is Barnum Road. Drive about two miles on this paved road and you will be in the tiny village of Barnum, West Virginia. This road takes you into a parking lot. To fish the upper one mile catch-and-release stretch, walk upriver, and you will run into an obvious path. This parallels the river for about 1/2 mile and then joins with an old railroad bed, which parallels the river the rest of the way. To get to the water near the upper end, walk in from little Lynn Run. Do not continue on the railroad bed, for entrance to the river from that point on is quite steep.

Summer trout tribulation in the North Branch Delayed Harvest Area. River warms and trout congregate at the mouth of a cool feeder stream.

From the parking lot we just mentioned, a dirt road parallels the entire put-and-take area downriver all the way to another parking lot and a closed gate, which is right below the giant Blue Hole. This begins the lower catch-and-release stretch. A railroad bed parallels it for its entire 4-mile stretch. You can walk this comfortable bed, or bike it.

The longer but easier way is as follows: Continue on Route 135, as above, to Route 38 and then to the town of Kitzmiller. Cross the river into West Virginia and continue to the town of Elk Garden. At the school in this town, go left onto Route 46, and stay on this past the reservoir. Continue to the churches and make a left onto Barnum Road. Follow as above.

To the Upper North Branch: The thing to remember is that getting to this section is a matter of traveling on dirt and gravel roads in the "back country." The delayed harvest section can be most readily accessed from Lostland Run Road and Wallman Road. To get to the Lostland Run Road area from I-68, take exit 19, Route 495 south for 20 miles to Swanton. Take a right at the stop sign in Swanton (still 495). At first blinking light, 495 changes to Route 136. Continue to town of Loch Lynn Heights and take a left at the stop light onto Route 560. Go about two miles to Bethlehem Road and turn left. Follow the Potomac State Forest signs. Continue two miles on Bethlehem Road to the first intersection. Go right (still Bethlehem Road) and continue for 1.5 miles and turn left onto Combination Road.

Continue 0.5 miles and turn left onto Potomac Camp Road. Pass the State Forest Headquarters about 0.5 miles and turn right onto a dirt road, which is Lostland Run Road. Follow this road to a parking area at the river. A path follows the river upstream for about 50 yards to a fork. Stay left and you will be to Lostland Run in a few yards. This feeder enters the river in a short distance. If the river is crossable when you fish it, you can also cross to the railroad tracks, and walk up or down them along the river looking for fishing possibilities.

To get to the Wallman area, you can also continue on Route 560 about three miles past Bethlehem Road. Turn left onto White Church-Steyer Road, and go a mile to Audley Riley Road. Stay on Audley Riley Road to a fork and bear right at Wallman Road. Continue two and three-quarter miles to a parking area near the river. The road parallels the river for a few miles upriver. Park at a pullover, and walk down to the river. You can take the railroad tracks up or down river from this point, and hike down from the tracks to the river.

Bibliography

Russell, Ed (1996). Maryland's North Branch of the Potomac. *Fly Fisherman*, 20 (#4), pp. 64-67, 81-85.

Russell, Ed (1997). Eastern Cutthroats? *American Angler*, 20 (#2), 82-85, 88-89.

CHAPTER 13
BEYOND THE USUAL

B elow are fly patterns that we have found to be highly effective in Maryland fishing. The majority of these will not ordinarily be found in fly shops or catalogues. We have originated some of these patterns and written about most of them in published articles. Having these patterns in your fly box might give you the advantage all fly anglers seek.

Sheppard's Patuxent Special

HOOK:	Mustad 9672 (streamer), sizes 6-12
THREAD:	Black, size 6/0
TAIL:	Fox squirrel tail
BODY:	Ginger chenille, weighted
HACKLE:	Ginger (palmered), 2-3X hook gap

This fly was originated by master fly tyer and guide Jay Sheppard. It has been one of the best all around flies we have fished. Jay created it for the purpose of imitating the crawfish.

Flourescent Woolly Bugger

HOOK:	Mustad 9672 or 79581, sizes 6-10
THREAD:	Black, size 6/0
TAIL:	Black marabou
BODY:	Fluorescent chartreuse, red, orange or yellow chenille
HACKLE:	Black (palmered)

Larry created this spin off of the traditional black Woolly Bugger. The Woolly Bugger is a fly that everyone should carry in his or her fly box because of its effectiveness. Changing the body color can give an angler an extra edge.

Little Black Stonefly

HOOK: Mustad 94840 (Dry), sizes 16-20
THREAD: Black, size 6/0
BODY: Black dry fly dubbing
WING: Grey duck quill
HACKLE: Black

The Little Black Stonefly is an excellent pattern for winter. Black stoneflies hatch from late Fall through the end of March.

Brown Stonefly

HOOK: Mustad 94840 (Dry), sizes 14-16
THREAD: Brown, size 6/0
BODY: Brown dry fly dubbing
WING: Mottled turkey quill
HACKLE: Brown

The brown stonefly is a hatch that shows up in the latter part of winter, although we have seen the insect reveal itself in February when the temperatures were right. Larry created the fly for imitating this particular insect.

Simple Three Hackle

HOOK: Mustad 94840 (Dry), sizes 16-22
                 or Partridge Captain Hamilton
                 L3A, sizes 20-24
THREAD: Black, size 6/0
TAIL/BODY: Hackle barb (Three small
                 clumps of brown, grizzly and
                 dun)
HACKLE: Grizzly, brown, and dun

Back in the early 1980s Jeff Mottern of Harrisburg, Pennsylvania created this fly to trick finicky trout of the Yellow Breeches. His tie was mainly in size 22. David Haidack of Potomac, Maryland expanded on the fly by tying it in sizes 14-24. It has become an excellent fly for difficult trout.

Charlie's Nymph

HOOK: Mustad 94840, sizes 16-20
THREAD: Black, size 6/0
BODY: Black Haretron dubbing
RIBBING: Gold wire or crystal flash
THORAX: Black Haretron dubbing
WING CASE: Black swiss straw
TAIL: 2 strands of black crystal flash
Note: Coat wing case with Dave's flex cement
    and pick dubbing from thorax for legs.

Charlie created a fly that would imitate the nymphal stage of the black winter stone fly. This nymph is very effective when stone flies become active. It is also useful when fish are taking other small, dark nymphs.

Little Marryat

HOOK: Mustad 94840, sizes 16-18
THREAD: Yellow or orange, size 6/0
TAIL: Mallard or wood duck flank
BODY: Pale yellow or sulphur orange
               dubbing
WING: Two cream or light dun mallard
               quill slips, tied wet fly style
HACKLE: Light dun or cream hen hackle,
    tied wet fly style

The Little Marryat is a traditional wet fly, which is a style of fly that has become less popular among today's anglers. But don't delete the wet fly from your arsenal, especially the Little Marryat during the sulphur hatch. This pattern is especially effective when the trout are not feeding on the surface.

Coburn's Sub-Surface Sulphur

HOOK: Mustad 94840 or 94833,
sizes 14-18
THREAD: Yellow, size 6/0
TAIL: Cream hackle barbs
BODY: Sulphur yellow Hareline dubbing
WING: Light gray duck quill
HEAD: Yellow foam

Fishing the sulphur hatch on the Gunpowder River is challenging because, after a few days of hard fishing pressure, the trout wise up to the traditional sulphur dry fly. Larry created this pattern that floats in the surface film, imitating a drowned dun. The sub-surface sulphur will trick fish that regularly refuse traditional dry flies.

REALISTIC CADDIS

When you need a caddis pattern to be as realistic as possible, all the patterns mentioned below will give you that advantage. All patterns are tied with mallard or turkey quill wings and 2-3 turns of hackle in the thorax area.

American Grannon

HOOK: Mustad 94833, sizes 12-16
THREAD: Color to match, size 6/0
BODY: Bright green to green-brown
dry fly dubbing
WING: Brown-gray mallard or turkey
LEGS: Dark brown hackle

Spotted Sedge

HOOK: Mustad 94833, sizes 12-16
THREAD: Color to match, size 6/0
BODY: Light olive to brown-yellow or
cinnamon dubbing
WING: Gray-brown mottled mallard
or turkey
LEGS: Brown or dun hackle

Green Sedge

HOOK: Mustad 94833, sizes 14-18
THREAD: Color to match, size 6/0
BODY: Olive dubbing
WING: Mottled gray-brown mallard or turkey
LEGS: Brown hackle

Dark Blue Sedge

HOOK: Mustad 94833, sizes 14-18
THREAD: Color to match, size 6/0
BODY: Dark green dry fly dubbing
WING: Dark gray mallard
LEGS: Brown or gray hackle

Little Black Sedge

HOOK: Mustad 94833, sizes 16-18
THREAD: Color to match, size 6/0
BODY: Black to black-brown dubbing
WING: Black mallard or turkey
LEGS: Black

MIDGES

Below is a system of midge patterns that should cover all midge-fishing conditions.

Stripped Peacock Herl Midge

HOOK: Mustad 94840 (Dry), size 20-28
THREAD: Black, size 6/0 or 8/0
TAIL: Couple of barbs of dark
              dun hackle
BODY: Stripped peacock herl
HACKLE: Dun

The stripped peacock herl midge has been a great producer on the surface when fish became selective.

Griffith Gnat

> HOOK: Mustad 94840 (Dry), sizes 20-28
> THREAD: Black, size 6/0 or 8/0
> BODY: Peacock herl
> HACKLE: Grizzly (palmered)

Griffith Gnat is an all around favorite dry fly when midges are hatching in large numbers. One thing that makes this fly so effective is that it imitates clustered midges. This occurs when a bunch of males try to mate with one female and end up on the surface of the water, creating a cluster. Also a great imitation of a fluttering midge.

Vertical Midge

> HOOK: 94840 Mustad, sizes 20-26
> THREAD: Black, size 6/0 or 8/0
> BODY: Stripped peacock herl
> THORAX: Gray dubbing
> WING: White poly yarn or floating foam

The vertical midge has become one of our favorites when the trout won't take the adult version on the surface. This fly imitates the midge when it is hatching in the surface film.

Simple Midge Pupa

> HOOK: 94840 Mustad, sizes 20-28
> THEAD: Black, size 6/0 or 8/0
> BODY: Stripped peacock herl
> THORAX: Gray dubbing

The midge pupa is a simple fly but a producer when you have to fish under the surface during the midge hatch. We also have caught many trout on this fly when the fish were deep.

Midge Serendipity

HOOK: Mustad 94840, sizes 20-28

THREAD: Black, size 6/0 or 8/0

TRAILING SHUCK: A few strands of
     zylon or wood duck flank

BODY: A few strands of zylon twisted
    and tightly wrapped, or stripped
    peacock herl.

WING: Bleached deer hair tied down-
    wing style and clipped to about
    a third the length of the shank.

Fish in the film or below. Trout seem to respond to this dynamite pattern as an emerging pupa or drowned midge adult.

Appendix

Below are listed some phone numbers and internet addresses that will be useful to the angler. They provide fishing reports and information on stream flows.

Phone Numbers

North Branch of the Potomac River: **410-962-7687**.
Provides water release in terms of cfs. from the Jennings-Randolph Dam.

Savage River: **410-962-7687**.
Gives water release in terms of cfs. from the Savage River Dam.

Youghiogheny River: **814-533-8911**.
Gives daily and weekly water discharge information from Deep Creek Lake into the Yock.

Gunpowder River: **410-329-6821**.
Phone number for On-the-Fly, a quality fly shop on the Gunpowder River that offers up-to-date stream information.

Internet URL Addresses

Department of Natural Resources: **http://www.dnr/state/md/us**
This is the main web page for the DNR.

DNR Fishing Report: **http://dnr.state.md.us/fisheries**
Weekly summary of fishing on Maryland streams and other waters.

USGS stream information: **http://md.usgs.gov/rt-cgi/gen_tbl_pg**
Much daily and weekly information on flows and gauge height for a few Maryland rivers.

US Army Corps of Engineers: **http://nab71.nab-wc.usace.army.mil**
Much information on the North Branch and the Savage.

Gunpowder River: **http://www.onthefly.com/fishrpt.html**
Fishing report on the Gunpowder River

ABOUT THE AUTHORS

Charlie Gelso and Larry Coburn have both been fly fishing and studying Maryland streams for over 20 years. Although their passion for the "gentle sport"

has taken them to many far away waters, their true love is Maryland trout streams. They have contributed to Maryland fishing in many ways, ranging from conservation efforts, to stocking local streams, to sitting on state committees aimed at enhancing fishing.

Charlie Gelso

Charlie and Larry are fly fishing guides, and both are also avid fly tyers and instructors, having created and written about several new patterns. Over the years, they have given many talks and classes throughout the state on tying and fishing, and have published often in top fly fishing magazines on

Larry Coburn

a range of topics, e.g., fly patterns and techniques for difficult trout, midge fishing, Maryland rivers and streams.

Larry owned *Laurel Fishing and Hunting* for several years, and Charlie has been a professor of psychology at the University of Maryland, he says, "from the beginning of time." Both reside in Laurel, Maryland.